The Epic Outdoor Griddle Cookbook

Over 150 Delicious Recipes, Plus Sauces and Marinades for Your Outdoor Griddle Cooking Adventures

Paul Gibbs

Copyright © 2024 - All rights reserved.

The content contained within this book may not be reproduced, duplicated, or transmitted without direct written permission from the author or the publisher.

Under no circumstances will any blame or legal responsibility be held against the publisher, or author, for any damages, reparation, or monetary loss due to the information contained within this book. Either directly or indirectly.

Legal Notice:

This book is copyright protected. This book is only for personal use. You cannot amend, distribute, sell, use, quote, or paraphrase any part, or the content within this book, without the consent of the author or publisher.

Disclaimer Notice:

Please note the information contained within this document is for educational and entertainment purposes only. All effort has been executed to present accurate, up-to-date, and reliable, complete information. No warranties of any kind are declared or implied. Readers acknowledge that the author is not engaging in the rendering of legal, financial, medical, or professional advice. The content within this book has been derived from various sources. Please consult a licensed professional before attempting any techniques outlined in this book.

By reading this document, the reader agrees that under no circumstances is the author responsible for any losses, direct or indirect, which are incurred as a result of the use of the information contained within this document, including, but not limited to, — errors, omissions, or inaccuracies.

Table of Contents:

- Introduction 1
- **Chapter 1: Preparation and Maintenance** 3
  - **Choosing and Installing the Perfect Grill** 3
  - **Maintenance and Cleaning** 5
- **Chapter 2: Grilling Techniques** 8
  - **Griddle Fundamentals** 8
  - **Pro Secrets** 10
- **Chapter 3: Unforgettable Breakfasts** 12
- **Perfect Pancakes** 12
  - **1. Classic Buttermilk Pancakes** 13
  - **2. Blueberry Pancakes** 13
  - **3. Banana Pancakes** 14
  - **4. Chocolate Chip Pancakes** 15
  - **5. Oatmeal Pancakes** 15
  - **6. Pumpkin Pancakes** 16
- **Grilled Eggs** 17
  - **7. Classic Fried Eggs** 17
  - **8. Cheesy Scrambled Eggs** 18
  - **9. Egg and Vegetable Skillet** 19
  - **10. Bacon and Egg Breakfast Sandwich** 19
  - **11. Spanish Tortilla** 20
  - **12. Avocado and Egg Breakfast Bowl** 21
- **Gourmet Sandwiches and Toasts** 21
  - **13. Avocado Toast with Poached Eggs** 21
  - **14. Caprese Breakfast Sandwich** 22
  - **15. Smoked Salmon and Cream Cheese Bagel** 23
  - **16. Bacon, Egg, and Cheese Breakfast Sandwich** 23
  - **17. Mediterranean Veggie Toast** 24
  - **18. Spicy Chorizo Breakfast Burrito** 25
  - **19. French Toast with Berries** 25
  - **20. Mushroom and Spinach Breakfast Wrap** 26
- **Chapter 4: Easy Lunches and Dinners** 27
- **Gourmet Burgers and Creative Hot Dogs** 27

21. Classic Cheeseburger 27
22. BBQ Bacon Burger 28
23. Guacamole Burger 29
24. Mushroom Swiss Burger 30
25. Spicy Jalapeño Burger 30
26. Teriyaki Pineapple Burger 31
27. Greek Lamb Burger 32
28. Chili Cheese Dog 33
29. Italian Sausage Dog 34
30. Hawaiian Hot Dog 34
31. Mexican Street Corn Dog 35
32. Buffalo Chicken Dog 36

Grilled Chicken and Fish 37

33. Lemon Herb Grilled Chicken 37
34. Teriyaki Grilled Chicken 37
35. Mediterranean Grilled Chicken 38
36. Honey Mustard Grilled Chicken 39
37. Cajun Grilled Chicken 39
38. Lemon Dill Grilled Salmon 40
39. Spicy Grilled Shrimp 41
40. Garlic Butter Grilled Tilapia 41
41. Herb Crusted Grilled Cod 42
42. Pesto Grilled Chicken 43

Chapter 5: Vegetarian Recipes 43

Grilled Vegetarian Dishes 43

43. Grilled Zucchini 44
44. Grilled Asparagus 44
45. Grilled Bell Peppers 45
46. Grilled Eggplant 45
47. Grilled Portobello Mushrooms 46
48. Grilled Corn on the Cob 47
49. Grilled Tomatoes 47
50. Grilled Carrots 48
51. Grilled Portobello Mushrooms 48
52. Grilled Vegetable Skewers 49
53. Grilled Eggplant Parmesan 50
54. Grilled Halloumi and Vegetable Platter 51
55. Grilled Corn and Black Bean Salad 51
56. Grilled Stuffed Bell Peppers 52

- 57. Grilled Cauliflower Steaks ... 53
- 58. Grilled Vegetable Pizza ... 54
- 59. Grilled Sweet Potato Wedges ... 55
- 60. Grilled Caprese Salad ... 55
- 61. Grilled Tofu Steaks ... 56
- 62. Grilled Tempeh Kebabs ... 57
- 63. Grilled Chickpea Patties ... 58
- 64. Grilled Seitan Cutlets ... 58
- 65. Grilled Black Bean Burgers ... 59
- 66. Grilled Lentil Sliders ... 60
- 67. Grilled Veggie Sausages ... 61
- 68. Grilled Falafel Patties ... 61
- 69. Grilled Quinoa-Stuffed Bell Peppers ... 62
- 70. Grilled Mushroom and Spinach Quesadillas ... 63

Chapter 6: Complete Meals for Every Occasion ... 64

Succulent Meats ... 64

- 71. Classic Grilled Ribeye Steak ... 64
- 72. BBQ Baby Back Ribs ... 65
- 73. Herb-Crusted Lamb Chops ... 65
- 74. Teriyaki Grilled Pork Tenderloin ... 66
- 75. Honey Garlic Chicken Thighs ... 67
- 76. Grilled Beef Kebabs ... 67
- 77. Spicy Grilled Sausages ... 68
- 78. Garlic Rosemary Grilled Pork Chops ... 69
- 79. Grilled Turkey Burgers ... 69
- 80. Grilled Lamb Skewers ... 70
- 81. Grilled BBQ Chicken ... 71
- 82. Grilled Beef Tenderloin ... 71

Refined Seafood Dishes ... 72

- 83. Grilled Shrimp Scampi ... 72
- 84. Grilled Lobster Tails ... 73
- 85. Grilled Scallops with Lemon Butter ... 73
- 86. Grilled Mahi Mahi with Pineapple Salsa ... 74
- 87. Grilled Swordfish Steaks ... 75
- 88. Grilled Tuna Steaks with Avocado Salsa ... 75
- 89. Grilled Clams with Garlic Butter ... 76
- 90. Grilled Calamari with Lemon and Herbs ... 77
- 91. Grilled Salmon with Dill Sauce ... 77
- 92. Grilled Tilapia with Mango Salsa ... 78

Irresistible Sides 79

93. Garlic Parmesan Grilled Potatoes 79
94. Grilled Asparagus with Lemon Zest 80
95. Grilled Corn on the Cob with Chili Lime Butter 80
96. Grilled Brussels Sprouts with Balsamic Glaze 81
97. Grilled Sweet Potato Wedges 81
98. Grilled Zucchini and Squash 82
99. Grilled Mushrooms with Thyme 83
100. Grilled Eggplant with Mint Yogurt Sauce 83

Chapter 7: International Cuisine on the Grill 84

Mexican Recipes 84

101. Grilled Chicken Tacos 84
102. Carne Asada 85
103. Grilled Fish Tacos 86
104. Grilled Street Corn (Elote) 87
105. Grilled Shrimp Fajitas 88
106. Grilled Quesadillas 88
107. Grilled Mexican Street Tacos 89
108. Grilled Jalapeño Poppers 90

Italian Recipes 91

109. Grilled Margherita Pizza 91
110. Grilled Chicken Alfredo 92
111. Grilled Caprese Salad 92
112. Grilled Italian Sausage and Peppers 93
113. Grilled Eggplant Parmesan 94
114. Grilled Bruschetta 95
115. Grilled Prosciutto-Wrapped Asparagus 95
116. Grilled Balsamic Chicken 96

Asian Recipes 97

117. Grilled Teriyaki Chicken Skewers 97
118. Grilled Miso Salmon 98
119. Grilled Thai Beef Salad 98
120. Grilled Soy-Ginger Shrimp 99
121. Grilled Korean BBQ Short Ribs (Galbi) 100
122. Grilled Tandoori Chicken 101
123. Grilled Teriyaki Pineapple Pork Chops 102
124. Grilled Vietnamese Pork Banh Mi 102

Fusion and Innovation 103

125. Korean BBQ Tacos 103
126. Teriyaki Chicken Quesadillas 104
127. Mediterranean BBQ Pizza 105
128. Thai Peanut Chicken Skewers 106
129. BBQ Pork Banh Mi Sandwich 107
130. Spicy Tandoori Fish Tacos 108

Chapter 8: Grilled Desserts 109

Grilled Fruits and Desserts 109

131. Grilled Pineapple with Cinnamon Sugar 109
132. Grilled Peaches with Honey and Mascarpone 110
133. Grilled Bananas with Chocolate Sauce 110
134. Grilled Apple Slices with Caramel Sauce 111
135. Grilled Strawberries with Balsamic Glaze 111
136. Grilled Pound Cake with Berries 112

Gourmet Sweets 113

137. Grilled S'mores 113
138. Grilled Lemon Pound Cake with Blueberry Compote 113
139. Grilled Mango with Lime and Chili 114
140. Grilled Chocolate-Dipped Strawberries 115
141. Grilled Pineapple Sundaes 115
142. Grilled Peaches with Amaretto 116
143. Grilled Apple Crisp 116
144. Grilled Banana Splits 117
145. Grilled Figs with Goat Cheese and Honey 118
146. Grilled Pears with Gorgonzola and Walnuts 118
147. Grilled Plums with Honey and Almonds 119
148. Grilled Nectarines with Ricotta and Honey 119
149. Grilled Pineapple and Coconut Rum Cake 120
150. Grilled Watermelon with Feta and Mint 121
151. Grilled Ananas with Ice Cream and Caramel Sauce 121

Chapter 8: Irresistible Sauces and Marinades 122

Sauces 122

1. Classic BBQ Sauce 122
2. Chimichurri Sauce 123
3. Honey Mustard Sauce 123
4. Spicy Sriracha Mayo 124
5. Teriyaki Sauce 124
6. Tzatziki Sauce 125

- 7. Mango Salsa 125
- 8. Garlic Herb Butter 126
- 9. Pesto Sauce 127
- 10. Lemon Dill Sauce 127

Marinades 128
- 1. Classic Italian Marinade 128
- 2. Spicy Chipotle Marinade 128
- 3. Asian Sesame Marinade 129
- 4. Mediterranean Lemon Marinade 130
- 5. Sweet and Tangy Teriyaki Marinade 130
- 6. Garlic Herb Marinade 131
- 7. Jamaican Jerk Marinade 131
- 8. Balsamic Rosemary Marinade 132
- 9. Smoky Paprika Marinade 132
- 10. Thai Coconut Marinade 133

Appendix 134

Conclusion 137

Introduction

Welcome to the World of Gas Grilling

Welcome to the exciting world of gas grilling! Whether you're a seasoned pro or a complete beginner, this book is your ultimate guide to mastering the art of grilling on a gas griddle. Gas grilling offers a unique blend of convenience, precision, and flavor that can elevate your cooking to new heights. Unlike charcoal grills, gas griddles heat up quickly, maintain a consistent temperature, and are easier to clean, making them perfect for any grilling enthusiast.

Imagine waking up on a weekend morning and effortlessly whipping up a gourmet breakfast on your gas griddle. Or hosting a summer barbecue where you can confidently serve perfectly grilled steaks, juicy burgers, and a variety of delicious sides. With the right techniques and recipes, your gas griddle can become the centerpiece of your culinary adventures.

In this book, you'll discover a wealth of recipes that cover everything from breakfast to dessert. Each recipe is designed to be easy to follow and packed with flavor. But this book is more than just a collection of recipes. It's a comprehensive guide that includes tips and tricks from grilling experts, advice on choosing and maintaining your griddle, and insights into the best grilling techniques. So, fire up your gas griddle, grab your favorite ingredients, and get ready to embark on a delicious journey!

The Journey to Mastery

Embarking on the journey to becoming a gas griddle master is both exciting and rewarding. It's a journey filled with discovery, creativity, and delicious food. Here's how this book will guide you along the way:

1. **Getting Started:** We'll begin with the basics. You'll learn how to choose the right gas griddle for your needs, set it up safely, and maintain it to ensure long-lasting performance. Proper setup and maintenance are the foundation of great grilling.

2. **Mastering Techniques:** Next, we'll dive into essential grilling techniques. From controlling the heat to achieving the perfect sear, these techniques will help you cook like a pro. You'll learn how to grill different types of food, including meats, vegetables, and even fruits. Each technique is explained in simple, easy-to-follow steps.

3. **Exploring Recipes:** This book is packed with over 150 mouthwatering recipes, each carefully crafted to make the most of your gas griddle. You'll find a wide range of dishes, including:

- **Unforgettable Breakfasts:** Start your day with perfect pancakes, gourmet sandwiches, and more.
- **Easy Lunches and Dinners:** Discover recipes for gourmet burgers, succulent meats, and delicious sides.
- **International Cuisine:** Travel the world with recipes inspired by Mexican, Italian, and Asian cuisines.
- **Grilled Desserts:** Satisfy your sweet tooth with innovative desserts cooked right on your griddle.
- **Vegetarian Options:** Enjoy a variety of flavorful vegetarian dishes that even meat lovers will appreciate.

4. **Beyond the Recipes:** In addition to recipes, you'll find valuable tips on grilling accessories, safety practices, and troubleshooting common issues. There's also a section dedicated to sauces and marinades that can elevate your dishes to new levels of flavor.

By the end of this book, you'll have all the knowledge and skills you need to become a true gas griddle master. You'll be able to impress your family and friends with delicious, perfectly cooked meals, and you'll enjoy the process every step of the way. So, let's get started on this flavorful journey together!

Chapter 1: Preparation and Maintenance

Choosing and Installing the Perfect Grill

Choosing the right gas griddle is the first step to becoming a griddle master. Here's what you need to consider:

1. **Size and Space**: Think about how much space you have and how many people you typically cook for. A larger griddle is great for big gatherings, but a smaller one might be better if you're cooking for just a few people or have limited space.

2. **Features**: Look for features like adjustable heat zones, a built-in thermometer, and a grease management system. These can make your grilling experience much easier and more enjoyable.

3. **Quality and Durability**: Invest in a high-quality griddle made from durable materials like stainless steel. It might cost a bit more upfront, but it will last longer and perform better.

Once you've chosen your griddle, it's time to set it up:

1. **Location**: Place your griddle in a well-ventilated area, away from any flammable materials. Make sure it's on a stable, flat surface.

2. **Gas Connection**: Follow the manufacturer's instructions to connect your griddle to a propane tank or natural gas line. Check for leaks by applying a soapy water solution to the connections and looking for bubbles.

3. **Initial Burn-Off**: Before cooking for the first time, perform an initial burn-off. Turn on the griddle to high heat for about 15-20 minutes. This will burn off any manufacturing residues and prepare the surface for cooking.

Maintenance and Cleaning

Keeping your gas griddle clean and well-maintained is crucial for great cooking results and longevity. Here's how to do it:

1. **After Each Use**:
    - **Scrape the Surface**: Use a griddle scraper to remove food particles and grease after each use.

- **Wipe Down**: Once the griddle has cooled slightly, wipe it down with a paper towel or a cloth. You can use a little water to help with this, but avoid using soap as it can strip the seasoning.
- **Oil the Surface**: Apply a thin layer of oil to the surface after cleaning. This helps maintain the seasoning and prevent rust.

2. **Deep Cleaning**: Perform a deep clean periodically, especially if you notice a buildup of grease or food particles.
   - **Heat and Scrape**: Turn the griddle on high to loosen any stubborn residue, then scrape it off.
   - **Use a Griddle Stone**: For tougher spots, use a griddle stone or pad to scrub the surface. Avoid using harsh chemicals or abrasive materials that can damage the griddle.
   - **Clean the Grease Trap**: Don't forget to empty and clean the grease trap regularly.

3. **Seasoning the Griddle**: Keeping your griddle well-seasoned is key to non-stick cooking and preventing rust.
   - **Initial Seasoning**: When you first get your griddle, or if it's been a while since you used it, you'll need to season it. Heat the griddle on high, then apply a thin layer of high-heat oil (like vegetable or canola oil). Spread it evenly with a cloth or paper towel, and let it heat until the oil starts to smoke. Repeat this process 2-3 times.
   - **Regular Maintenance**: After each use and cleaning, apply a thin layer of oil to keep the surface seasoned.

4. **Storage**: Proper storage will extend the life of your griddle.
   - **Cover It Up**: Use a cover to protect your griddle from the elements when it's not in use.
   - **Store Indoors**: If possible, store your griddle indoors during the off-season or if you don't plan to use it for an extended period.

5. **Check for Wear and Tear**: Regularly inspect your griddle for any signs of wear or damage.
   - **Burners and Hoses**: Check the burners and gas hoses for blockages or leaks. Replace any damaged parts immediately.

- **Ignition System**: Make sure the ignition system is working properly. Clean any dirt or debris that might be affecting its performance.

By following these preparation and maintenance tips, you'll ensure that your gas griddle stays in top condition and is always ready to deliver delicious meals. Proper care not only enhances your cooking experience but also extends the life of your equipment, making it a worthy investment for any grilling enthusiast.

Maintenance and Cleaning

Maintaining and cleaning your gas griddle is essential for ensuring its longevity and keeping it in top working condition. A well-maintained griddle not only performs better but also enhances the flavor of your food. Here's a detailed guide on how to care for your gas griddle.

After Each Use

1. **Scrape the Surface**:
    - **Tools**: Use a griddle scraper or spatula designed for high heat to remove food particles and excess grease. Scrape the griddle surface while it's still warm, as food residue comes off more easily.
    - **Technique**: Hold the scraper at a slight angle and push it firmly across the surface. Work from back to front, moving the debris into the grease trap.

2. **Wipe Down**:
    - **Cloth or Paper Towel**: Once the griddle has cooled slightly, use a damp cloth or paper towel to wipe down the surface. This helps remove any remaining food particles and grease.
    - **Avoid Soap**: Avoid using soap, as it can strip the seasoning from the griddle. If you need to use a cleaner, choose one specifically designed for griddles.

3. **Oil the Surface**:
    - **Thin Layer of Oil**: After wiping down the griddle, apply a thin layer of high-heat oil to the surface. This helps maintain the seasoning and prevents rust.
    - **Spread Evenly**: Use a paper towel or cloth to spread the oil evenly across the griddle.

Deep Cleaning

Perform a deep clean periodically, especially if you notice a buildup of grease or food particles.

1. **Heat and Scrape**:
    - **High Heat**: Turn the griddle on high to loosen any stubborn residue. Heat for about 10 minutes.
    - **Scrape Thoroughly**: Use a scraper to remove the loosened residue. Be thorough, ensuring you get into all the corners and edges.

2. **Use a Griddle Stone or Pad**:
    - **Griddle Stone**: For tougher spots, use a griddle stone or pad. These tools help remove stuck-on food without damaging the surface.
    - **Scrub Gently**: Scrub gently but firmly, focusing on areas with the most buildup. Rinse with water to remove debris as you go.

3. **Grease Trap**:
    - **Empty Regularly**: Empty and clean the grease trap regularly. Built-up grease can cause flare-ups and affect the griddle's performance.
    - **Clean Thoroughly**: Remove the trap, empty it, and clean it with warm, soapy water. Rinse and dry before reinserting it.

Seasoning the Griddle

Seasoning is essential for creating a non-stick surface and protecting your griddle from rust.

1. **Initial Seasoning**:
    - **Clean Surface**: Start with a clean griddle surface. Perform an initial burn-off to remove any residues.
    - **Apply Oil**: Apply a thin layer of high-heat oil to the griddle surface. Spread it evenly using a cloth or paper towel.
    - **Heat**: Turn on the griddle to high heat until the oil starts to smoke. Turn off the heat and let it cool. Repeat this process 2-3 times to build a good seasoning layer.

2. **Regular Maintenance**:
    - **Post-Cooking**: After each use and cleaning, apply a thin layer of oil to maintain the seasoning.

- **Periodic Re-seasoning**: If food starts sticking or the surface looks dry and dull, repeat the initial seasoning process.

Storage

Proper storage will protect your griddle and keep it in prime condition.

1. **Cover It Up**:
    - **Protective Cover**: Use a high-quality cover to protect your griddle from dust, moisture, and other elements when not in use.
    - **Fitted Cover**: Ensure the cover fits well to provide full protection.
2. **Store Indoors**:
    - **Indoor Storage**: If possible, store your griddle indoors during the off-season or if you don't plan to use it for an extended period. This will protect it from harsh weather and extend its lifespan.

Check for Wear and Tear

Regularly inspect your griddle for any signs of wear or damage.

1. **Burners and Hoses**:
    - **Check for Blockages**: Ensure the burners are free of blockages and the hoses are intact. Replace any damaged parts immediately.
    - **Leak Test**: Perform a leak test periodically, especially after reconnecting the gas supply.
2. **Ignition System**:
    - **Clean and Inspect**: Clean the ignition system and inspect it for any signs of wear. Ensure it's functioning properly to avoid any starting issues.

By following these maintenance and cleaning tips, you'll ensure that your gas griddle remains in excellent condition, providing you with delicious meals for years to come. Regular care and proper storage are key to enjoying the best grilling experience possible.

Chapter 2: Grilling Techniques

Griddle Fundamentals

Grilling on a gas griddle can be simple and rewarding once you understand the basics. Here's everything you need to know to get started and achieve consistently great results.

Heat Control

1. **Preheating**:

    - **Why It's Important**: Preheating ensures that the cooking surface is evenly heated, which helps cook food more evenly.

    - **How to Do It**: Turn on your griddle to medium-high heat and let it preheat for about 10-15 minutes. You can test the heat by sprinkling a few drops of water on the surface – they should sizzle and evaporate quickly.

2. **Adjusting Heat Zones**:

    - **Multiple Zones**: Use different heat zones to cook various foods simultaneously. For instance, you can have one side of the griddle on high heat for searing and the other on low for warming or cooking delicate items.

    - **Heat Distribution**: Ensure you understand your griddle's heat distribution, as some areas might get hotter than others. Adjust your cooking positions accordingly.

Cooking Techniques

1. **Searing**:

    - **What It Is**: Searing involves cooking food at high temperatures to create a caramelized crust.

    - **How to Do It**: Preheat the griddle to high heat. Add a thin layer of oil, then place the food on the griddle. Don't move it until it forms a crust, then flip it to sear the other side.

2. **Direct Grilling**:

    - **What It Is**: Cooking food directly over the heat source.

- **How to Do It**: Place food directly on the griddle surface over the burners. This method is great for burgers, steaks, and vegetables. Keep an eye on the food and flip it as needed to ensure even cooking.

3. **Indirect Grilling**:
   - **What It Is**: Cooking food adjacent to the heat source rather than directly over it.
   - **How to Do It**: Use indirect grilling for larger cuts of meat that require longer cooking times. Preheat one side of the griddle to medium-high heat and keep the other side off or on low. Place the food on the cooler side and close the lid if your griddle has one.

4. **Stir-Frying**:
   - **What It Is**: Quickly cooking small, uniform pieces of food in a small amount of oil over high heat.
   - **How to Do It**: Preheat the griddle to high heat and add a thin layer of oil. Add the food and stir continuously with a spatula to ensure even cooking. This method is perfect for vegetables, shrimp, and thinly sliced meats.

Essential Tips

1. **Oil Management**:
   - **Types of Oil**: Use oils with high smoke points like vegetable, canola, or peanut oil.
   - **Applying Oil**: Use a paper towel or brush to apply a thin, even layer of oil to the griddle before cooking. This prevents sticking and helps with even browning.

2. **Monitoring Food**:
   - **Visual Cues**: Look for changes in color and texture to judge doneness. For example, meat juices should run clear when fully cooked.
   - **Internal Temperatures**: Use a meat thermometer to check the internal temperature of meats to ensure they are cooked to a safe level.

3. **Using the Right Tools**:
   - **Spatulas**: Use metal spatulas with a flat edge to flip and move food easily.

- o **Tongs**: Tongs are great for handling larger items like steaks or chicken breasts.
- o **Thermometer**: A good meat thermometer is essential for checking doneness.

4. **Resting Meat**:
   - o **Why It's Important**: Letting meat rest after cooking allows the juices to redistribute, resulting in more flavorful and moist meat.
   - o **How to Do It**: Remove the meat from the griddle and let it rest on a plate, covered loosely with foil, for about 5-10 minutes.

By mastering these griddle fundamentals, you'll be well on your way to grilling like a pro. Understanding heat control, cooking techniques, and essential tips will help you achieve delicious, consistent results every time you fire up your gas griddle.

Pro Secrets

Now that you have the basics down, it's time to take your grilling skills to the next level with some pro secrets. These tips and tricks will help you refine your technique and impress your guests with your culinary prowess.

Perfecting the Sear

1. **Pat Dry**:
   - o **Why It's Important**: Moisture on the surface of your food can prevent proper searing.
   - o **How to Do It**: Before placing meat on the griddle, pat it dry with paper towels. This helps achieve a better sear and a more flavorful crust.

2. **Seasoning**:
   - o **Timing**: Season meat just before placing it on the griddle. Salt draws out moisture, so salting too early can lead to a less effective sear.
   - o **Even Coverage**: Apply seasoning evenly across the surface for balanced flavor.

3. **Oil Before Searing**:
   - o **Light Coat**: Apply a light coat of high-smoke-point oil directly to the meat before searing. This helps achieve a better crust and prevents sticking.

Advanced Techniques

1. **Reverse Searing**:
   - **What It Is**: Cooking meat slowly at a low temperature first, then searing it at high heat to finish.
   - **How to Do It**: Cook the meat on the cooler side of the griddle or in the oven at a low temperature until it's almost done. Then, move it to the high-heat side of the griddle for a quick sear to finish.

2. **Using a Press**:
   - **What It Is**: Using a grill press or a heavy pan to apply pressure while cooking.
   - **How to Do It**: Pressing burgers or sandwiches helps achieve an even sear and cooks the food more quickly. Just place the press on top of the food and apply gentle pressure.

3. **Basting**:
   - **What It Is**: Adding moisture and flavor to food by brushing it with a liquid during cooking.
   - **How to Do It**: Use a brush or spoon to apply butter, oil, or a marinade to the food as it cooks. This keeps it moist and enhances the flavor.

Flavor Enhancements

1. **Marinades and Brines**:
   - **Why They Work**: Marinades and brines add flavor and moisture to meat.
   - **How to Do It**: Marinate meat for at least 30 minutes to overnight, depending on the recipe. Brining, especially for poultry, can be done for a few hours to a day.

2. **Compound Butters**:
   - **What They Are**: Flavored butters that can be added to meat after cooking.
   - **How to Do It**: Mix softened butter with herbs, spices, and other flavorings. Place a dollop on hot meat just before serving for an extra burst of flavor.

3. **Smoke Infusion**:
   - **What It Is**: Adding smoky flavor to food even on a gas griddle.
   - **How to Do It**: Use a smoking box with wood chips on the griddle, or add a few drops of liquid smoke to marinades and sauces.

Troubleshooting

1. **Avoiding Flare-Ups**:
   - **Why They Happen**: Flare-ups occur when fat drips onto the heat source.
   - **How to Prevent**: Trim excess fat from meat and use a drip tray. If a flare-up occurs, move the food to a cooler part of the griddle until it subsides.

2. **Even Cooking**:
   - **Hot Spots**: Be aware of hot spots on your griddle and move food around to ensure even cooking.
   - **Temperature Control**: Use different heat zones and adjust the burners as needed to maintain consistent cooking temperatures.

3. **Sticking Issues**:
   - **Prevention**: Ensure your griddle is well-seasoned and oiled before cooking. Avoid moving food too soon – let it form a crust before flipping.
   - **Solution**: If food sticks, use a spatula to gently release it without tearing.

By incorporating these pro secrets into your grilling routine, you'll enhance your skills and produce even more impressive dishes. Whether you're searing a perfect steak, experimenting with advanced techniques, or adding new layers of flavor, these tips will help you cook like a true grill master.

Chapter 3: Unforgettable Breakfasts

Perfect Pancakes

Pancakes are a breakfast staple, and cooking them on a gas griddle ensures they come out perfectly every time. Here are six delicious pancake recipes to start your day right.

1. Classic Buttermilk Pancakes

Ingredients:

- 2 cups all-purpose flour
- 2 tablespoons sugar
- 2 teaspoons baking powder
- 1 teaspoon baking soda
- 1/2 teaspoon salt
- 2 cups buttermilk
- 2 large eggs
- 1/4 cup melted butter
- Butter or oil for griddle

Instructions:

1. **Mix Dry Ingredients**: In a large bowl, whisk together the flour, sugar, baking powder, baking soda, and salt.
2. **Combine Wet Ingredients**: In another bowl, whisk the buttermilk, eggs, and melted butter.
3. **Combine Wet and Dry**: Pour the wet ingredients into the dry ingredients and stir until just combined. Do not overmix; lumps are okay.
4. **Preheat Griddle**: Heat the griddle to medium heat and lightly grease with butter or oil.
5. **Cook Pancakes**: Pour 1/4 cup of batter onto the griddle for each pancake. Cook until bubbles form on the surface and edges look set, about 2-3 minutes. Flip and cook for another 1-2 minutes until golden brown.
6. **Serve**: Serve hot with butter and syrup.

2. Blueberry Pancakes

Ingredients:

- Same ingredients as Classic Buttermilk Pancakes
- 1 cup fresh or frozen blueberries

Instructions:

1. **Prepare Batter**: Follow steps 1-3 from the Classic Buttermilk Pancakes recipe.
2. **Add Blueberries**: Gently fold in the blueberries into the batter.
3. **Preheat Griddle**: Heat the griddle to medium heat and lightly grease with butter or oil.
4. **Cook Pancakes**: Pour 1/4 cup of batter onto the griddle for each pancake. Cook until bubbles form on the surface and edges look set, about 2-3 minutes. Flip and cook for another 1-2 minutes until golden brown.
5. **Serve**: Serve hot with butter and syrup.

3. Banana Pancakes

Ingredients:

- Same ingredients as Classic Buttermilk Pancakes
- 2 ripe bananas, mashed
- 1 teaspoon vanilla extract

Instructions:

1. **Prepare Batter**: Follow steps 1-3 from the Classic Buttermilk Pancakes recipe, adding the mashed bananas and vanilla extract to the wet ingredients.
2. **Combine**: Mix the wet and dry ingredients until just combined.
3. **Preheat Griddle**: Heat the griddle to medium heat and lightly grease with butter or oil.
4. **Cook Pancakes**: Pour 1/4 cup of batter onto the griddle for each pancake. Cook until bubbles form on the surface and edges look set, about 2-3 minutes. Flip and cook for another 1-2 minutes until golden brown.
5. **Serve**: Serve hot with butter, syrup, and additional banana slices if desired.

4. Chocolate Chip Pancakes

Ingredients:

- Same ingredients as Classic Buttermilk Pancakes
- 1 cup chocolate chips

Instructions:

1. **Prepare Batter**: Follow steps 1-3 from the Classic Buttermilk Pancakes recipe.
2. **Add Chocolate Chips**: Gently fold in the chocolate chips into the batter.
3. **Preheat Griddle**: Heat the griddle to medium heat and lightly grease with butter or oil.
4. **Cook Pancakes**: Pour 1/4 cup of batter onto the griddle for each pancake. Cook until bubbles form on the surface and edges look set, about 2-3 minutes. Flip and cook for another 1-2 minutes until golden brown.
5. **Serve**: Serve hot with butter and syrup.

5. Oatmeal Pancakes

Ingredients:

- 1 cup rolled oats
- 1 1/2 cups buttermilk
- 1 cup all-purpose flour
- 2 tablespoons sugar
- 1 teaspoon baking powder
- 1 teaspoon baking soda
- 1/2 teaspoon salt
- 2 large eggs
- 1/4 cup melted butter
- Butter or oil for griddle

Instructions:

1. **Soak Oats**: In a bowl, combine the rolled oats and buttermilk. Let sit for 10 minutes.
2. **Mix Dry Ingredients**: In another bowl, whisk together the flour, sugar, baking powder, baking soda, and salt.
3. **Combine Wet Ingredients**: Add the eggs and melted butter to the oats and buttermilk mixture.
4. **Combine Wet and Dry**: Pour the wet ingredients into the dry ingredients and stir until just combined.
5. **Preheat Griddle**: Heat the griddle to medium heat and lightly grease with butter or oil.
6. **Cook Pancakes**: Pour 1/4 cup of batter onto the griddle for each pancake. Cook until bubbles form on the surface and edges look set, about 2-3 minutes. Flip and cook for another 1-2 minutes until golden brown.
7. **Serve**: Serve hot with butter and syrup.

6. Pumpkin Pancakes

Ingredients:

- 1 1/2 cups all-purpose flour
- 2 tablespoons sugar
- 2 teaspoons baking powder
- 1 teaspoon baking soda
- 1/2 teaspoon salt
- 1 teaspoon ground cinnamon
- 1/2 teaspoon ground ginger
- 1/4 teaspoon ground nutmeg
- 1 cup buttermilk
- 1 cup pumpkin puree
- 2 large eggs

- 1/4 cup melted butter
- Butter or oil for griddle

Instructions:

1. **Mix Dry Ingredients**: In a large bowl, whisk together the flour, sugar, baking powder, baking soda, salt, cinnamon, ginger, and nutmeg.
2. **Combine Wet Ingredients**: In another bowl, whisk the buttermilk, pumpkin puree, eggs, and melted butter.
3. **Combine Wet and Dry**: Pour the wet ingredients into the dry ingredients and stir until just combined. Do not overmix; lumps are okay.
4. **Preheat Griddle**: Heat the griddle to medium heat and lightly grease with butter or oil.
5. **Cook Pancakes**: Pour 1/4 cup of batter onto the griddle for each pancake. Cook until bubbles form on the surface and edges look set, about 2-3 minutes. Flip and cook for another 1-2 minutes until golden brown.
6. **Serve**: Serve hot with butter and syrup.

These six pancake recipes will turn your breakfasts into unforgettable meals. With classic flavors and some unique twists, you'll have the perfect pancakes for any occasion.

Grilled Eggs

Grilling eggs on a gas griddle brings out a delightful flavor and texture that's hard to achieve with traditional cooking methods. Here are six delicious grilled egg recipes to start your day off right.

7. Classic Fried Eggs

Ingredients:

- 4 large eggs

- Salt and pepper, to taste
- Butter or oil for the griddle

Instructions:

1. **Preheat Griddle**: Heat the griddle to medium heat and lightly grease with butter or oil.
2. **Crack Eggs**: Crack the eggs directly onto the griddle.
3. **Cook Eggs**: Cook until the whites are set and the yolks are cooked to your desired doneness, about 3-4 minutes for sunny-side-up. For over-easy, flip the eggs gently and cook for an additional 1-2 minutes.
4. **Season**: Sprinkle with salt and pepper.
5. **Serve**: Serve hot with toast or your favorite breakfast sides.

8. Cheesy Scrambled Eggs

Ingredients:

- 6 large eggs
- 1/4 cup milk
- 1/2 cup shredded cheddar cheese
- Salt and pepper, to taste
- Butter or oil for the griddle

Instructions:

1. **Mix Eggs**: In a bowl, whisk together the eggs, milk, salt, and pepper.
2. **Preheat Griddle**: Heat the griddle to medium heat and lightly grease with butter or oil.
3. **Cook Eggs**: Pour the egg mixture onto the griddle. Let it sit for a few seconds, then gently stir with a spatula.
4. **Add Cheese**: Sprinkle the cheese over the eggs and continue cooking until the eggs are just set but still soft.
5. **Serve**: Serve immediately with toast or other breakfast favorites.

9. Egg and Vegetable Skillet

Ingredients:

- 4 large eggs
- 1 cup diced bell peppers
- 1 cup diced onions
- 1 cup diced tomatoes
- Salt and pepper, to taste
- Butter or oil for the griddle

Instructions:

1. **Cook Vegetables**: Preheat the griddle to medium heat and lightly grease with butter or oil. Add the bell peppers, onions, and tomatoes. Cook until softened, about 5 minutes.
2. **Add Eggs**: Crack the eggs directly onto the griddle, nestling them among the vegetables.
3. **Cook Eggs**: Cook until the whites are set and the yolks are cooked to your liking, about 3-4 minutes.
4. **Season**: Sprinkle with salt and pepper.
5. **Serve**: Serve hot, directly from the griddle.

10. Bacon and Egg Breakfast Sandwich

Ingredients:

- 4 large eggs
- 4 slices of bacon
- 4 slices of cheddar cheese
- 4 English muffins, split and toasted
- Salt and pepper, to taste
- Butter or oil for the griddle

Instructions:

1. **Cook Bacon**: Preheat the griddle to medium heat and cook the bacon until crispy. Remove and set aside.

2. **Cook Eggs**: Crack the eggs onto the griddle and cook until the whites are set, about 3-4 minutes. For over-easy eggs, flip and cook for an additional minute.

3. **Assemble Sandwiches**: Place a slice of cheese on the bottom half of each English muffin. Top with a cooked egg, a slice of bacon, and the top half of the muffin.

4. **Serve**: Serve hot with your favorite breakfast sides.

11. Spanish Tortilla

Ingredients:

- 6 large eggs
- 2 cups thinly sliced potatoes
- 1 cup diced onions
- Salt and pepper, to taste
- Olive oil for the griddle

Instructions:

1. **Cook Potatoes and Onions**: Preheat the griddle to medium heat and lightly grease with olive oil. Add the potatoes and onions, cooking until tender and golden brown, about 10 minutes.

2. **Mix Eggs**: In a bowl, whisk the eggs with salt and pepper.

3. **Combine**: Pour the egg mixture over the potatoes and onions on the griddle.

4. **Cook Tortilla**: Let cook until the eggs are set and the bottom is golden brown, about 5-7 minutes. Carefully flip the tortilla using a large spatula and cook for another 3-4 minutes.

5. **Serve**: Slice into wedges and serve hot.

12. Avocado and Egg Breakfast Bowl

Ingredients:

- 4 large eggs
- 2 avocados, halved and pitted
- 1 cup cherry tomatoes, halved
- 1/4 cup crumbled feta cheese
- Salt and pepper, to taste
- Olive oil for the griddle

Instructions:

1. **Cook Eggs**: Preheat the griddle to medium heat and lightly grease with olive oil. Crack the eggs onto the griddle and cook until the whites are set, about 3-4 minutes.
2. **Prepare Avocados**: While the eggs are cooking, scoop the avocado halves into bowls.
3. **Assemble Bowls**: Place a cooked egg into each avocado half. Top with cherry tomatoes and crumbled feta cheese.
4. **Season**: Sprinkle with salt and pepper.
5. **Serve**: Serve immediately, with additional toppings if desired.

These six grilled egg recipes are versatile and delicious, perfect for a hearty breakfast or brunch. Enjoy experimenting with different ingredients and flavors to make these dishes your own.

Gourmet Sandwiches and Toasts

Sandwiches and toasts are quick, versatile breakfast options that can be easily customized. Here are eight gourmet recipes that will elevate your morning meals.

13. Avocado Toast with Poached Eggs

Ingredients:

- 4 slices of whole grain bread

- 2 ripe avocados
- 4 large eggs
- 1 tablespoon vinegar
- Salt and pepper, to taste
- Red pepper flakes, for garnish

Instructions:

1. **Toast Bread**: Preheat the griddle to medium heat. Lightly butter the bread slices and toast them on the griddle until golden brown, about 2-3 minutes per side.
2. **Mash Avocado**: In a bowl, mash the avocados with a fork. Season with salt and pepper.
3. **Poach Eggs**: Bring a pot of water to a simmer and add the vinegar. Crack each egg into a small bowl, then gently slide them into the water. Cook for about 3-4 minutes, or until the whites are set.
4. **Assemble Toasts**: Spread the mashed avocado on each toast. Top with a poached egg.
5. **Serve**: Sprinkle with red pepper flakes and serve immediately.

14. Caprese Breakfast Sandwich

Ingredients:

- 4 English muffins, split and toasted
- 8 slices of fresh mozzarella
- 8 slices of tomato
- Fresh basil leaves
- Balsamic glaze
- Salt and pepper, to taste

Instructions:

1. **Toast Muffins**: Preheat the griddle to medium heat and toast the English muffins until golden brown, about 2 minutes per side.

2. **Assemble Sandwiches**: Place two slices of mozzarella on the bottom half of each muffin. Top with two slices of tomato and a few basil leaves.

3. **Season**: Drizzle with balsamic glaze and sprinkle with salt and pepper.

4. **Serve**: Place the top half of the muffin on each sandwich and serve immediately.

15. Smoked Salmon and Cream Cheese Bagel

Ingredients:

- 4 bagels, split and toasted
- 8 ounces cream cheese, softened
- 8 slices of smoked salmon
- 1 small red onion, thinly sliced
- Capers, for garnish
- Fresh dill, for garnish

Instructions:

1. **Toast Bagels**: Preheat the griddle to medium heat and toast the bagels until golden brown, about 2 minutes per side.

2. **Spread Cream Cheese**: Spread a generous amount of cream cheese on each bagel half.

3. **Add Salmon**: Layer two slices of smoked salmon on top of the cream cheese.

4. **Garnish**: Top with red onion slices, capers, and fresh dill.

5. **Serve**: Serve immediately.

16. Bacon, Egg, and Cheese Breakfast Sandwich

Ingredients:

- 4 croissants, split
- 8 slices of bacon
- 4 large eggs

- 4 slices of cheddar cheese
- Salt and pepper, to taste
- Butter or oil for the griddle

Instructions:

1. **Cook Bacon**: Preheat the griddle to medium heat and cook the bacon until crispy. Remove and set aside.
2. **Cook Eggs**: Crack the eggs onto the griddle and cook until the whites are set, about 3-4 minutes. For over-easy eggs, flip and cook for an additional minute.
3. **Assemble Sandwiches**: Place a slice of cheddar cheese on the bottom half of each croissant. Top with an egg, two slices of bacon, and the top half of the croissant.
4. **Serve**: Serve hot.

17. Mediterranean Veggie Toast

Ingredients:

- 4 slices of sourdough bread
- 1 cup hummus
- 1 cucumber, thinly sliced
- 1 red bell pepper, thinly sliced
- 1/4 cup crumbled feta cheese
- Fresh parsley, for garnish

Instructions:

1. **Toast Bread**: Preheat the griddle to medium heat. Lightly butter the bread slices and toast them on the griddle until golden brown, about 2-3 minutes per side.
2. **Spread Hummus**: Spread a generous layer of hummus on each toast.
3. **Add Veggies**: Top with cucumber slices, red bell pepper slices, and crumbled feta cheese.
4. **Garnish**: Sprinkle with fresh parsley.

5. **Serve**: Serve immediately.

18. Spicy Chorizo Breakfast Burrito

Ingredients:

- 4 large flour tortillas
- 8 ounces chorizo, crumbled
- 6 large eggs
- 1 cup shredded cheddar cheese
- 1 cup diced tomatoes
- 1 avocado, diced
- Salsa, for serving
- Butter or oil for the griddle

Instructions:

1. **Cook Chorizo**: Preheat the griddle to medium heat and cook the chorizo until browned and crispy. Remove and set aside.
2. **Scramble Eggs**: In a bowl, whisk the eggs with salt and pepper. Pour onto the griddle and cook, stirring occasionally, until just set.
3. **Assemble Burritos**: Place a tortilla on the griddle to warm. Add a portion of scrambled eggs, chorizo, shredded cheddar, diced tomatoes, and avocado.
4. **Roll Burritos**: Roll up the tortilla, folding in the sides to enclose the filling.
5. **Serve**: Serve with salsa.

19. French Toast with Berries

Ingredients:

- 4 slices of brioche or thick bread
- 4 large eggs

- 1 cup milk
- 1 teaspoon vanilla extract
- 1/2 teaspoon ground cinnamon
- Butter or oil for the griddle
- Fresh berries (strawberries, blueberries, raspberries)
- Maple syrup, for serving

Instructions:

1. **Prepare Egg Mixture**: In a bowl, whisk together the eggs, milk, vanilla extract, and cinnamon.
2. **Dip Bread**: Dip each slice of bread into the egg mixture, ensuring both sides are well-coated.
3. **Cook Bread**: Preheat the griddle to medium heat and lightly grease with butter or oil. Cook the bread slices until golden brown, about 2-3 minutes per side.
4. **Serve**: Top with fresh berries and maple syrup. Serve immediately.

20. Mushroom and Spinach Breakfast Wrap

Ingredients:

- 4 large whole wheat tortillas
- 1 cup sliced mushrooms
- 2 cups fresh spinach
- 6 large eggs
- 1/2 cup shredded mozzarella cheese
- Salt and pepper, to taste
- Butter or oil for the griddle

Instructions:

1. **Cook Vegetables**: Preheat the griddle to medium heat. Cook the mushrooms until softened, about 5 minutes. Add the spinach and cook until wilted, about 2 minutes.

2. **Scramble Eggs**: In a bowl, whisk the eggs with salt and pepper. Pour onto the griddle and cook, stirring occasionally, until just set.

3. **Assemble Wraps**: Place a tortilla on the griddle to warm. Add a portion of scrambled eggs, cooked mushrooms, spinach, and shredded mozzarella.

4. **Roll Wraps**: Roll up the tortilla, folding in the sides to enclose the filling.

5. **Serve**: Serve immediately.

These eight gourmet sandwiches and toasts offer a variety of flavors and ingredients to keep your breakfasts exciting and delicious. Enjoy experimenting with these recipes and making them your own!

Chapter 4: Easy Lunches and Dinners

Gourmet Burgers and Creative Hot Dogs

Burgers and hot dogs are classic favorites that can be easily elevated with some creative touches. Here are twelve delicious recipes to try on your gas griddle.

21. Classic Cheeseburger

Ingredients:

- 1 lb ground beef (80/20 blend)
- 4 slices of cheddar cheese
- 4 hamburger buns
- Salt and pepper, to taste
- Butter or oil for the griddle
- Lettuce, tomato, pickles, ketchup, and mustard for toppings

Instructions:

1. **Form Patties**: Divide the ground beef into four equal portions and shape into patties. Season both sides with salt and pepper.

2. **Preheat Griddle**: Heat the griddle to medium-high heat and lightly grease with butter or oil.

3. **Cook Patties**: Place the patties on the griddle and cook for 3-4 minutes per side, or until they reach your desired doneness. Place a slice of cheese on each patty during the last minute of cooking to melt.

4. **Toast Buns**: While the patties cook, toast the buns on the griddle until golden brown.

5. **Assemble Burgers**: Place each patty on the bottom half of a bun and add your favorite toppings. Cover with the top bun and serve hot.

22. BBQ Bacon Burger

Ingredients:

- 1 lb ground beef (80/20 blend)
- 4 slices of pepper jack cheese
- 4 hamburger buns
- 8 slices of bacon
- 1/2 cup BBQ sauce
- Salt and pepper, to taste
- Butter or oil for the griddle
- Lettuce, tomato, and pickles for toppings

Instructions:

1. **Form Patties**: Divide the ground beef into four equal portions and shape into patties. Season both sides with salt and pepper.

2. **Cook Bacon**: Preheat the griddle to medium heat and cook the bacon until crispy. Remove and set aside.

3. **Cook Patties**: Increase the griddle to medium-high heat and cook the patties for 3-4 minutes per side, or until desired doneness. Add a slice of pepper jack cheese to each patty during the last minute of cooking to melt.

4. **Toast Buns**: Toast the buns on the griddle until golden brown.

5. **Assemble Burgers**: Spread BBQ sauce on the bottom half of each bun. Add the patty, bacon slices, and toppings. Cover with the top bun and serve hot.

---

23. Guacamole Burger

Ingredients:

- 1 lb ground beef (80/20 blend)
- 4 slices of Monterey Jack cheese
- 4 hamburger buns
- 1 cup guacamole
- Salt and pepper, to taste
- Butter or oil for the griddle
- Lettuce, tomato, and red onion for toppings

Instructions:

1. **Form Patties**: Divide the ground beef into four equal portions and shape into patties. Season both sides with salt and pepper.

2. **Preheat Griddle**: Heat the griddle to medium-high heat and lightly grease with butter or oil.

3. **Cook Patties**: Cook the patties for 3-4 minutes per side, or until they reach your desired doneness. Place a slice of Monterey Jack cheese on each patty during the last minute of cooking to melt.

4. **Toast Buns**: Toast the buns on the griddle until golden brown.

5. **Assemble Burgers**: Spread guacamole on the bottom half of each bun. Add the patty and toppings. Cover with the top bun and serve hot.

24. Mushroom Swiss Burger

Ingredients:

- 1 lb ground beef (80/20 blend)
- 4 slices of Swiss cheese
- 4 hamburger buns
- 1 cup sliced mushrooms
- 1 tablespoon butter
- Salt and pepper, to taste
- Butter or oil for the griddle

Instructions:

1. **Form Patties**: Divide the ground beef into four equal portions and shape into patties. Season both sides with salt and pepper.
2. **Cook Mushrooms**: Preheat the griddle to medium heat and melt the butter. Add the mushrooms and cook until softened, about 5 minutes. Remove and set aside.
3. **Cook Patties**: Increase the griddle to medium-high heat and cook the patties for 3-4 minutes per side, or until desired doneness. Add a slice of Swiss cheese to each patty during the last minute of cooking to melt.
4. **Toast Buns**: Toast the buns on the griddle until golden brown.
5. **Assemble Burgers**: Place each patty on the bottom half of a bun, top with cooked mushrooms, and cover with the top bun. Serve hot.

25. Spicy Jalapeño Burger

Ingredients:

- 1 lb ground beef (80/20 blend)
- 4 slices of pepper jack cheese
- 4 hamburger buns

- 1/4 cup pickled jalapeños
- 1/2 cup spicy mayo (mix mayonnaise with sriracha)
- Salt and pepper, to taste
- Butter or oil for the griddle

Instructions:

1. **Form Patties**: Divide the ground beef into four equal portions and shape into patties. Season both sides with salt and pepper.
2. **Preheat Griddle**: Heat the griddle to medium-high heat and lightly grease with butter or oil.
3. **Cook Patties**: Cook the patties for 3-4 minutes per side, or until they reach your desired doneness. Place a slice of pepper jack cheese on each patty during the last minute of cooking to melt.
4. **Toast Buns**: Toast the buns on the griddle until golden brown.
5. **Assemble Burgers**: Spread spicy mayo on the bottom half of each bun. Add the patty, pickled jalapeños, and top with the bun. Serve hot.

26. Teriyaki Pineapple Burger

Ingredients:

- 1 lb ground beef (80/20 blend)
- 4 slices of provolone cheese
- 4 hamburger buns
- 4 pineapple rings
- 1/4 cup teriyaki sauce
- Salt and pepper, to taste
- Butter or oil for the griddle

- Lettuce and red onion for toppings

Instructions:

1. **Form Patties**: Divide the ground beef into four equal portions and shape into patties. Season both sides with salt and pepper.

2. **Preheat Griddle**: Heat the griddle to medium-high heat and lightly grease with butter or oil.

3. **Cook Patties**: Cook the patties for 3-4 minutes per side, or until they reach your desired doneness. Brush with teriyaki sauce during the last minute of cooking. Place a slice of provolone cheese on each patty to melt.

4. **Grill Pineapple**: Place the pineapple rings on the griddle and cook until lightly charred, about 2 minutes per side.

5. **Toast Buns**: Toast the buns on the griddle until golden brown.

6. **Assemble Burgers**: Place each patty on the bottom half of a bun, top with a grilled pineapple ring, and add lettuce and red onion. Cover with the top bun and serve hot.

27. Greek Lamb Burger

Ingredients:

- 1 lb ground lamb
- 4 ounces feta cheese, crumbled
- 4 hamburger buns
- 1/2 cup tzatziki sauce
- Salt, pepper, and dried oregano, to taste
- Butter or oil for the griddle
- Sliced cucumber and red onion for toppings

Instructions:

1. **Form Patties**: Mix the ground lamb with crumbled feta cheese, salt, pepper, and oregano. Divide into four equal portions and shape into patties.

2. **Preheat Griddle**: Heat the griddle to medium-high heat and lightly grease with butter or oil.

3. **Cook Patties**: Cook the patties for 3-4 minutes per side, or until they reach your desired doneness.

4. **Toast Buns**: Toast the buns on the griddle until golden brown.

5. **Assemble Burgers**: Spread tzatziki sauce on the bottom half of each bun. Add the lamb patty, cucumber slices, and red onion. Cover with the top bun and serve hot.

28. Chili Cheese Dog

Ingredients:

- 4 hot dogs
- 4 hot dog buns
- 1 cup prepared chili
- 1 cup shredded cheddar cheese
- Diced onions and jalapeños for garnish
- Butter or oil for the griddle

Instructions:

1. **Heat Chili**: Preheat the griddle to medium heat. Heat the prepared chili in a small saucepan on the griddle or nearby stovetop.

2. **Cook Hot Dogs**: Place the hot dogs on the griddle and cook until browned and heated through, about 5-7 minutes, turning occasionally.

3. **Toast Buns**: Toast the hot dog buns on the griddle until golden brown.

4. **Assemble Dogs**: Place each hot dog in a bun, top with hot chili, shredded cheddar cheese, and garnish with diced onions and jalapeños.

5. **Serve**: Serve hot.

29. Italian Sausage Dog

Ingredients:

- 4 Italian sausages
- 4 hoagie rolls
- 1 bell pepper, sliced
- 1 onion, sliced
- 1/2 cup marinara sauce
- Shredded mozzarella cheese
- Butter or oil for the griddle

Instructions:

1. **Cook Sausages**: Preheat the griddle to medium heat. Cook the Italian sausages until browned and cooked through, about 10-12 minutes, turning occasionally.
2. **Cook Peppers and Onions**: While the sausages cook, add the bell pepper and onion slices to the griddle. Cook until softened, about 5 minutes.
3. **Heat Marinara**: Heat the marinara sauce in a small saucepan on the griddle or nearby stovetop.
4. **Toast Rolls**: Toast the hoagie rolls on the griddle until golden brown.
5. **Assemble Dogs**: Place each sausage in a roll, top with cooked peppers and onions, a spoonful of marinara sauce, and shredded mozzarella cheese.
6. **Serve**: Serve hot.

30. Hawaiian Hot Dog

Ingredients:

- 4 hot dogs
- 4 hot dog buns
- 4 pineapple rings

- 1/4 cup teriyaki sauce
- Sliced green onions and sesame seeds for garnish
- Butter or oil for the griddle

Instructions:

1. **Grill Pineapple**: Preheat the griddle to medium heat and lightly grease with butter or oil. Grill the pineapple rings until lightly charred, about 2 minutes per side.
2. **Cook Hot Dogs**: Place the hot dogs on the griddle and cook until browned and heated through, about 5-7 minutes, turning occasionally.
3. **Brush with Teriyaki Sauce**: During the last minute of cooking, brush the hot dogs with teriyaki sauce.
4. **Toast Buns**: Toast the hot dog buns on the griddle until golden brown.
5. **Assemble Dogs**: Place each hot dog in a bun, top with a grilled pineapple ring, and garnish with sliced green onions and sesame seeds.
6. **Serve**: Serve hot.

31. Mexican Street Corn Dog

Ingredients:

- 4 hot dogs
- 4 hot dog buns
- 1/2 cup mayonnaise
- 1/2 cup crumbled cotija cheese
- 1 teaspoon chili powder
- 1 lime, cut into wedges
- Fresh cilantro, for garnish
- Butter or oil for the griddle

Instructions:

1. **Cook Hot Dogs**: Preheat the griddle to medium heat. Place the hot dogs on the griddle and cook until browned and heated through, about 5-7 minutes, turning occasionally.

2. **Toast Buns**: Toast the hot dog buns on the griddle until golden brown.

3. **Prepare Toppings**: Mix the mayonnaise with chili powder.

4. **Assemble Dogs**: Place each hot dog in a bun, spread with chili mayo, and top with crumbled cotija cheese. Garnish with fresh cilantro.

5. **Serve**: Serve with lime wedges on the side.

32. Buffalo Chicken Dog

Ingredients:

- 4 chicken sausages
- 4 hot dog buns
- 1/2 cup buffalo sauce
- 1/4 cup blue cheese crumbles
- 1/4 cup diced celery
- Butter or oil for the griddle

Instructions:

1. **Cook Sausages**: Preheat the griddle to medium heat. Cook the chicken sausages until browned and cooked through, about 8-10 minutes, turning occasionally.

2. **Brush with Buffalo Sauce**: During the last minute of cooking, brush the chicken sausages with buffalo sauce.

3. **Toast Buns**: Toast the hot dog buns on the griddle until golden brown.

4. **Assemble Dogs**: Place each sausage in a bun, sprinkle with blue cheese crumbles and diced celery.

5. **Serve**: Serve hot with additional buffalo sauce if desired.

These gourmet burgers and creative hot dogs offer a variety of flavors and ingredients that will elevate your lunch or dinner. Enjoy experimenting with these recipes and making them your own!

Grilled Chicken and Fish

Grilling chicken and fish on a gas griddle brings out their natural flavors and creates delicious, healthy meals. Here are ten recipes to try.

33. Lemon Herb Grilled Chicken

Ingredients:

- 4 boneless, skinless chicken breasts
- 1/4 cup olive oil
- Juice of 2 lemons
- 2 cloves garlic, minced
- 1 tablespoon fresh thyme, chopped
- 1 tablespoon fresh rosemary, chopped
- Salt and pepper, to taste

Instructions:

1. **Marinate Chicken**: In a bowl, mix olive oil, lemon juice, garlic, thyme, rosemary, salt, and pepper. Add the chicken breasts and marinate for at least 30 minutes.
2. **Preheat Griddle**: Heat the griddle to medium-high heat and lightly grease with olive oil.
3. **Grill Chicken**: Place the chicken on the griddle and cook for 6-7 minutes per side, or until fully cooked and juices run clear.
4. **Serve**: Serve hot with your favorite sides.

34. Teriyaki Grilled Chicken

Ingredients:

- 4 boneless, skinless chicken thighs
- 1/2 cup teriyaki sauce
- 1 tablespoon honey
- 1 teaspoon grated ginger
- 1 clove garlic, minced
- Sliced green onions and sesame seeds for garnish

Instructions:

1. **Marinate Chicken**: In a bowl, mix teriyaki sauce, honey, ginger, and garlic. Add the chicken thighs and marinate for at least 30 minutes.
2. **Preheat Griddle**: Heat the griddle to medium-high heat and lightly grease with oil.
3. **Grill Chicken**: Place the chicken on the griddle and cook for 5-6 minutes per side, or until fully cooked and juices run clear.
4. **Garnish and Serve**: Garnish with sliced green onions and sesame seeds. Serve hot.

35. Mediterranean Grilled Chicken

Ingredients:

- 4 boneless, skinless chicken breasts
- 1/4 cup olive oil
- Juice of 1 lemon
- 1 teaspoon dried oregano
- 1 teaspoon dried thyme
- 2 cloves garlic, minced
- Salt and pepper, to taste

Instructions:

1. **Marinate Chicken**: In a bowl, mix olive oil, lemon juice, oregano, thyme, garlic, salt, and pepper. Add the chicken breasts and marinate for at least 30 minutes.

2. **Preheat Griddle**: Heat the griddle to medium-high heat and lightly grease with olive oil.
3. **Grill Chicken**: Place the chicken on the griddle and cook for 6-7 minutes per side, or until fully cooked and juices run clear.
4. **Serve**: Serve hot with a side of Greek salad.

36. Honey Mustard Grilled Chicken

Ingredients:

- 4 boneless, skinless chicken breasts
- 1/4 cup honey
- 1/4 cup Dijon mustard
- 2 tablespoons olive oil
- 2 cloves garlic, minced
- Salt and pepper, to taste

Instructions:

1. **Marinate Chicken**: In a bowl, mix honey, Dijon mustard, olive oil, garlic, salt, and pepper. Add the chicken breasts and marinate for at least 30 minutes.
2. **Preheat Griddle**: Heat the griddle to medium-high heat and lightly grease with olive oil.
3. **Grill Chicken**: Place the chicken on the griddle and cook for 6-7 minutes per side, or until fully cooked and juices run clear.
4. **Serve**: Serve hot with roasted vegetables.

37. Cajun Grilled Chicken

Ingredients:

- 4 boneless, skinless chicken thighs
- 2 tablespoons olive oil
- 1 tablespoon Cajun seasoning

- 1 teaspoon smoked paprika
- Salt and pepper, to taste

Instructions:

1. **Season Chicken**: In a bowl, mix olive oil, Cajun seasoning, smoked paprika, salt, and pepper. Add the chicken thighs and coat evenly.
2. **Preheat Griddle**: Heat the griddle to medium-high heat and lightly grease with oil.
3. **Grill Chicken**: Place the chicken on the griddle and cook for 5-6 minutes per side, or until fully cooked and juices run clear.
4. **Serve**: Serve hot with rice or quinoa.

---

38. Lemon Dill Grilled Salmon

Ingredients:

- 4 salmon fillets
- 1/4 cup olive oil
- Juice of 1 lemon
- 1 tablespoon fresh dill, chopped
- 2 cloves garlic, minced
- Salt and pepper, to taste

Instructions:

1. **Marinate Salmon**: In a bowl, mix olive oil, lemon juice, dill, garlic, salt, and pepper. Add the salmon fillets and marinate for at least 15 minutes.
2. **Preheat Griddle**: Heat the griddle to medium-high heat and lightly grease with olive oil.

3. **Grill Salmon**: Place the salmon fillets on the griddle, skin side down. Cook for 4-5 minutes per side, or until the salmon is opaque and flakes easily with a fork.
4. **Serve**: Serve hot with a side of steamed vegetables.

39. Spicy Grilled Shrimp

Ingredients:

- 1 lb large shrimp, peeled and deveined
- 2 tablespoons olive oil
- 1 tablespoon hot sauce
- 1 teaspoon smoked paprika
- 2 cloves garlic, minced
- Salt and pepper, to taste
- Lemon wedges for serving

Instructions:

1. **Marinate Shrimp**: In a bowl, mix olive oil, hot sauce, smoked paprika, garlic, salt, and pepper. Add the shrimp and marinate for at least 15 minutes.
2. **Preheat Griddle**: Heat the griddle to medium-high heat and lightly grease with oil.
3. **Grill Shrimp**: Place the shrimp on the griddle and cook for 2-3 minutes per side, or until pink and opaque.
4. **Serve**: Serve hot with lemon wedges.

40. Garlic Butter Grilled Tilapia

Ingredients:

- 4 tilapia fillets
- 1/4 cup melted butter
- 2 cloves garlic, minced

- 1 tablespoon fresh parsley, chopped
- Salt and pepper, to taste
- Lemon wedges for serving

Instructions:

1. **Prepare Butter Mixture**: In a bowl, mix melted butter, garlic, parsley, salt, and pepper.
2. **Preheat Griddle**: Heat the griddle to medium-high heat and lightly grease with butter or oil.
3. **Grill Tilapia**: Brush the tilapia fillets with the garlic butter mixture and place on the griddle. Cook for 3-4 minutes per side, or until the fish is opaque and flakes easily with a fork.
4. **Serve**: Serve hot with lemon wedges.

41. Herb Crusted Grilled Cod

Ingredients:

- 4 cod fillets
- 1/4 cup olive oil
- 1/4 cup breadcrumbs
- 1 tablespoon fresh parsley, chopped
- 1 tablespoon fresh thyme, chopped
- 1 clove garlic, minced
- Salt and pepper, to taste
- Lemon wedges for serving

Instructions:

1. **Prepare Herb Crust**: In a bowl, mix olive oil, breadcrumbs, parsley, thyme, garlic, salt, and pepper.
2. **Preheat Griddle**: Heat the griddle to medium-high heat and lightly grease with olive oil.

3. **Grill Cod**: Press the breadcrumb mixture onto the cod fillets and place on the griddle. Cook for 4-5 minutes per side, or until the fish is opaque and flakes easily with a fork.
4. **Serve**: Serve hot with lemon wedges.

42. Pesto Grilled Chicken

Ingredients:

- 4 boneless, skinless chicken breasts
- 1/2 cup basil pesto
- Salt and pepper, to taste
- Cherry tomatoes and mozzarella balls for serving

Instructions:

1. **Marinate Chicken**: Coat the chicken breasts with basil pesto and season with salt and pepper. Marinate for at least 30 minutes.
2. **Preheat Griddle**: Heat the griddle to medium-high heat and lightly grease with oil.
3. **Grill Chicken**: Place the chicken on the griddle and cook for 6-7 minutes per side, or until fully cooked and juices run clear.
4. **Serve**: Serve hot with a side of cherry tomatoes and mozzarella balls.

These ten grilled chicken and fish recipes offer a variety of flavors and ingredients to create delicious, healthy meals for lunch or dinner. Enjoy experimenting with these recipes and making them your own!

Chapter 5: Vegetarian Recipes

Grilled Vegetarian Dishes

Vegetarian grilling can be just as flavorful and satisfying as meat-based dishes. Here are ten delicious grilled vegetarian recipes that will make your taste buds sing.

43. Grilled Zucchini

Ingredients:

- 4 zucchinis, sliced lengthwise
- 2 tablespoons olive oil
- 2 cloves garlic, minced
- Salt and pepper, to taste
- Fresh parsley, chopped, for garnish

Instructions:

1. **Prepare Zucchini**: In a bowl, toss the zucchini slices with olive oil, garlic, salt, and pepper.
2. **Preheat Griddle**: Heat the griddle to medium-high heat.
3. **Grill Zucchini**: Place the zucchini slices on the griddle and cook for 3-4 minutes per side, or until tender and slightly charred.
4. **Garnish and Serve**: Sprinkle with fresh parsley and serve hot.

44. Grilled Asparagus

Ingredients:

- 1 bunch of asparagus, trimmed
- 2 tablespoons olive oil
- 1 teaspoon lemon zest
- Salt and pepper, to taste
- Lemon wedges for serving

Instructions:

1. **Prepare Asparagus**: In a bowl, toss the asparagus with olive oil, lemon zest, salt, and pepper.

2. **Preheat Griddle**: Heat the griddle to medium-high heat.
3. **Grill Asparagus**: Place the asparagus on the griddle and cook for 2-3 minutes per side, or until tender and slightly charred.
4. **Serve**: Serve hot with lemon wedges.

45. Grilled Bell Peppers

Ingredients:

- 4 bell peppers (red, yellow, green), cut into quarters
- 2 tablespoons olive oil
- 1 teaspoon balsamic vinegar
- Salt and pepper, to taste
- Fresh basil, chopped, for garnish

Instructions:

1. **Prepare Bell Peppers**: In a bowl, toss the bell peppers with olive oil, balsamic vinegar, salt, and pepper.
2. **Preheat Griddle**: Heat the griddle to medium-high heat.
3. **Grill Bell Peppers**: Place the bell peppers on the griddle and cook for 4-5 minutes per side, or until tender and slightly charred.
4. **Garnish and Serve**: Sprinkle with fresh basil and serve hot.

46. Grilled Eggplant

Ingredients:

- 2 large eggplants, sliced into rounds
- 2 tablespoons olive oil
- 2 cloves garlic, minced
- Salt and pepper, to taste

- Fresh mint, chopped, for garnish

Instructions:

1. **Prepare Eggplant**: In a bowl, toss the eggplant slices with olive oil, garlic, salt, and pepper.

2. **Preheat Griddle**: Heat the griddle to medium-high heat.

3. **Grill Eggplant**: Place the eggplant slices on the griddle and cook for 3-4 minutes per side, or until tender and slightly charred.

4. **Garnish and Serve**: Sprinkle with fresh mint and serve hot.

47. Grilled Portobello Mushrooms

Ingredients:

- 4 large Portobello mushrooms, stems removed
- 2 tablespoons olive oil
- 1 tablespoon balsamic vinegar
- 1 teaspoon dried thyme
- Salt and pepper, to taste

Instructions:

1. **Prepare Mushrooms**: In a bowl, mix olive oil, balsamic vinegar, thyme, salt, and pepper. Brush the mixture onto the mushrooms.

2. **Preheat Griddle**: Heat the griddle to medium-high heat.

3. **Grill Mushrooms**: Place the mushrooms on the griddle, gill side down, and cook for 4-5 minutes per side, or until tender and slightly charred.

4. **Serve**: Serve hot as a side or use in sandwiches.

48. Grilled Corn on the Cob

Ingredients:

- 4 ears of corn, husked
- 2 tablespoons butter, melted
- 1 teaspoon smoked paprika
- Salt and pepper, to taste
- Fresh cilantro, chopped, for garnish

Instructions:

1. **Prepare Corn**: Brush the corn with melted butter and season with smoked paprika, salt, and pepper.
2. **Preheat Griddle**: Heat the griddle to medium-high heat.
3. **Grill Corn**: Place the corn on the griddle and cook for 10-12 minutes, turning occasionally, until the corn is tender and slightly charred.
4. **Garnish and Serve**: Sprinkle with fresh cilantro and serve hot.

49. Grilled Tomatoes

Ingredients:

- 4 large tomatoes, halved
- 2 tablespoons olive oil
- 2 cloves garlic, minced
- Salt and pepper, to taste
- Fresh basil, chopped, for garnish

Instructions:

1. **Prepare Tomatoes**: In a bowl, toss the tomato halves with olive oil, garlic, salt, and pepper.

2. **Preheat Griddle**: Heat the griddle to medium-high heat.

3. **Grill Tomatoes**: Place the tomatoes on the griddle, cut side down, and cook for 3-4 minutes per side, or until tender and slightly charred.

4. **Garnish and Serve**: Sprinkle with fresh basil and serve hot.

50. Grilled Carrots

Ingredients:

- 8 large carrots, peeled and halved lengthwise
- 2 tablespoons olive oil
- 1 tablespoon honey
- 1 teaspoon ground cumin
- Salt and pepper, to taste
- Fresh parsley, chopped, for garnish

Instructions:

1. **Prepare Carrots**: In a bowl, toss the carrots with olive oil, honey, cumin, salt, and pepper.

2. **Preheat Griddle**: Heat the griddle to medium-high heat.

3. **Grill Carrots**: Place the carrots on the griddle and cook for 4-5 minutes per side, or until tender and slightly charred.

4. **Garnish and Serve**: Sprinkle with fresh parsley and serve hot.

51. Grilled Portobello Mushrooms

Ingredients:

- 4 large portobello mushrooms

- 1/4 cup olive oil
- 2 tablespoons balsamic vinegar
- 2 cloves garlic, minced
- 1 teaspoon dried thyme
- Salt and pepper, to taste

Instructions:

1. **Prepare Marinade**: In a bowl, mix olive oil, balsamic vinegar, garlic, thyme, salt, and pepper.
2. **Marinate Mushrooms**: Brush the portobello mushrooms with the marinade and let sit for 15-20 minutes.
3. **Preheat Griddle**: Heat the griddle to medium-high heat.
4. **Grill Mushrooms**: Place the mushrooms on the griddle, gill side up, and cook for 5-7 minutes per side, until tender.
5. **Serve**: Serve hot as a main dish or sliced in a sandwich.

52. Grilled Vegetable Skewers

Ingredients:

- 1 zucchini, sliced into rounds
- 1 yellow squash, sliced into rounds
- 1 red bell pepper, cut into chunks
- 1 red onion, cut into chunks
- 1 cup cherry tomatoes
- 1/4 cup olive oil
- 2 tablespoons balsamic vinegar
- Salt and pepper, to taste
- Skewers

Instructions:

1. **Prepare Vegetables**: In a bowl, toss the vegetables with olive oil, balsamic vinegar, salt, and pepper.

2. **Assemble Skewers**: Thread the vegetables onto skewers, alternating colors.

3. **Preheat Griddle**: Heat the griddle to medium-high heat.

4. **Grill Skewers**: Place the skewers on the griddle and cook for 10-12 minutes, turning occasionally, until the vegetables are tender and slightly charred.

5. **Serve**: Serve hot as a main or side dish.

53. Grilled Eggplant Parmesan

Ingredients:

- 2 large eggplants, sliced into rounds
- 1/4 cup olive oil
- 1 cup marinara sauce
- 1 cup shredded mozzarella cheese
- 1/2 cup grated Parmesan cheese
- Fresh basil leaves for garnish
- Salt and pepper, to taste

Instructions:

1. **Prepare Eggplant**: Brush the eggplant slices with olive oil and season with salt and pepper.

2. **Preheat Griddle**: Heat the griddle to medium-high heat.

3. **Grill Eggplant**: Place the eggplant slices on the griddle and cook for 3-4 minutes per side, until tender and lightly charred.

4. **Assemble Parmesan**: Place grilled eggplant slices on a baking sheet, top with marinara sauce, mozzarella cheese, and Parmesan cheese.

5. **Melt Cheese**: Place the baking sheet under a broiler for 3-4 minutes, until the cheese is melted and bubbly.
6. **Garnish and Serve**: Garnish with fresh basil leaves and serve hot.

54. Grilled Halloumi and Vegetable Platter

Ingredients:

- 8 ounces halloumi cheese, sliced
- 1 zucchini, sliced lengthwise
- 1 red bell pepper, cut into strips
- 1 red onion, sliced into rings
- 1/4 cup olive oil
- 1 teaspoon dried oregano
- Salt and pepper, to taste
- Lemon wedges for serving

Instructions:

1. **Prepare Vegetables and Halloumi**: In a bowl, toss the vegetables and halloumi slices with olive oil, oregano, salt, and pepper.
2. **Preheat Griddle**: Heat the griddle to medium-high heat.
3. **Grill Vegetables and Halloumi**: Place the vegetables and halloumi on the griddle and cook for 3-4 minutes per side, until tender and lightly charred.
4. **Serve**: Serve the grilled vegetables and halloumi hot with lemon wedges.

55. Grilled Corn and Black Bean Salad

Ingredients:

- 4 ears of corn, husked

- 1 can black beans, drained and rinsed
- 1 red bell pepper, diced
- 1/4 cup red onion, diced
- 1/4 cup fresh cilantro, chopped
- 2 tablespoons olive oil
- Juice of 1 lime
- Salt and pepper, to taste

Instructions:

1. **Grill Corn**: Preheat the griddle to medium-high heat. Place the corn on the griddle and cook for 10-12 minutes, turning occasionally, until charred and tender.
2. **Prepare Salad**: Cut the kernels off the grilled corn and place in a bowl. Add black beans, red bell pepper, red onion, and cilantro.
3. **Dress Salad**: Drizzle with olive oil and lime juice, season with salt and pepper, and toss to combine.
4. **Serve**: Serve the salad cold or at room temperature.

56. Grilled Stuffed Bell Peppers

Ingredients:

- 4 bell peppers, tops cut off and seeds removed
- 1 cup cooked quinoa
- 1 can black beans, drained and rinsed
- 1 cup corn kernels
- 1 cup diced tomatoes
- 1 teaspoon ground cumin
- 1 teaspoon chili powder
- 1/4 cup shredded cheddar cheese

- Salt and pepper, to taste

Instructions:

1. **Prepare Filling**: In a bowl, mix cooked quinoa, black beans, corn, diced tomatoes, cumin, chili powder, salt, and pepper.

2. **Stuff Peppers**: Stuff each bell pepper with the quinoa mixture.

3. **Preheat Griddle**: Heat the griddle to medium-high heat.

4. **Grill Peppers**: Place the stuffed peppers on the griddle and cook for 15-20 minutes, until the peppers are tender and slightly charred.

5. **Add Cheese**: Sprinkle the tops with cheddar cheese and cook for an additional 5 minutes, until the cheese is melted.

6. **Serve**: Serve hot as a main dish.

57. Grilled Cauliflower Steaks

Ingredients:

- 1 large head of cauliflower, cut into thick steaks
- 1/4 cup olive oil
- 2 cloves garlic, minced
- 1 teaspoon smoked paprika
- Salt and pepper, to taste
- Fresh parsley, chopped, for garnish

Instructions:

1. **Prepare Cauliflower**: In a bowl, mix olive oil, garlic, smoked paprika, salt, and pepper. Brush the cauliflower steaks with the mixture.

2. **Preheat Griddle**: Heat the griddle to medium-high heat.

3. **Grill Cauliflower**: Place the cauliflower steaks on the griddle and cook for 5-7 minutes per side, until tender and charred.

4. **Garnish and Serve**: Sprinkle with fresh parsley and serve hot.

58. Grilled Vegetable Pizza

Ingredients:

- 1 lb pizza dough
- 1/2 cup marinara sauce
- 1 cup shredded mozzarella cheese
- 1 zucchini, sliced
- 1 yellow squash, sliced
- 1 red bell pepper, sliced
- 1/4 cup red onion, thinly sliced
- 2 tablespoons olive oil
- Salt and pepper, to taste

Instructions:

1. **Preheat Griddle**: Heat the griddle to medium-high heat and brush with olive oil.

2. **Grill Vegetables**: Place the zucchini, squash, and bell pepper slices on the griddle and cook for 3-4 minutes per side, until tender and lightly charred.

3. **Prepare Dough**: Roll out the pizza dough on a lightly floured surface.

4. **Grill Dough**: Place the dough on the griddle and cook for 2-3 minutes per side, until lightly browned and firm.

5. **Add Toppings**: Spread marinara sauce over the grilled dough, top with mozzarella cheese, grilled vegetables, and red onion.

6. **Finish Cooking**: Cover the griddle with a lid and cook for another 3-4 minutes, until the cheese is melted.

7. **Serve**: Serve hot, sliced into wedges.

59. Grilled Sweet Potato Wedges

Ingredients:

- 2 large sweet potatoes, cut into wedges
- 2 tablespoons olive oil
- 1 teaspoon smoked paprika
- 1 teaspoon ground cumin
- Salt and pepper, to taste
- Fresh parsley, chopped, for garnish

Instructions:

1. **Prepare Sweet Potatoes**: In a bowl, toss the sweet potato wedges with olive oil, smoked paprika, cumin, salt, and pepper.
2. **Preheat Griddle**: Heat the griddle to medium-high heat.
3. **Grill Sweet Potatoes**: Place the sweet potato wedges on the griddle and cook for 5-7 minutes per side, until tender and charred.
4. **Garnish and Serve**: Sprinkle with fresh parsley and serve hot.

60. Grilled Caprese Salad

Ingredients:

- 4 large tomatoes, sliced
- 8 ounces fresh mozzarella, sliced
- 1/4 cup fresh basil leaves
- 2 tablespoons olive oil
- Balsamic glaze, for drizzling

- Salt and pepper, to taste

Instructions:

1. **Preheat Griddle**: Heat the griddle to medium-high heat and lightly grease with olive oil.

2. **Grill Tomatoes**: Place the tomato slices on the griddle and cook for 2-3 minutes per side, until lightly charred.

3. **Assemble Salad**: Arrange grilled tomatoes and mozzarella slices on a serving platter. Top with fresh basil leaves.

4. **Season and Serve**: Drizzle with olive oil and balsamic glaze, sprinkle with salt and pepper, and serve.

These ten grilled vegetarian recipes are packed with flavor and perfect for any occasion. Enjoy these delicious and healthy dishes at your next barbecue or as a part of your regular meal rotation!

61. Grilled Tofu Steaks

Ingredients:

- 1 block firm tofu, pressed and sliced into 1-inch thick steaks
- 1/4 cup soy sauce
- 2 tablespoons olive oil
- 2 tablespoons maple syrup
- 1 teaspoon smoked paprika
- 2 cloves garlic, minced

Instructions:

1. **Prepare Marinade**: In a bowl, mix soy sauce, olive oil, maple syrup, smoked paprika, and garlic.

2. **Marinate Tofu**: Place tofu steaks in the marinade and let sit for at least 30 minutes.

3. **Preheat Griddle**: Heat the griddle to medium-high heat.

4. **Grill Tofu**: Place the tofu steaks on the griddle and cook for 3-4 minutes per side, until golden and slightly charred.
5. **Serve**: Serve hot with your favorite side dishes.

62. Grilled Tempeh Kebabs

Ingredients:

- 1 block tempeh, cut into 1-inch cubes
- 1/4 cup soy sauce
- 2 tablespoons maple syrup
- 1 tablespoon olive oil
- 1 teaspoon ground cumin
- 1 teaspoon smoked paprika
- 1 red bell pepper, cut into chunks
- 1 red onion, cut into chunks
- Skewers

Instructions:

1. **Prepare Marinade**: In a bowl, mix soy sauce, maple syrup, olive oil, cumin, and smoked paprika.
2. **Marinate Tempeh**: Place tempeh cubes in the marinade and let sit for at least 30 minutes.
3. **Assemble Kebabs**: Thread tempeh, red bell pepper, and red onion onto skewers.
4. **Preheat Griddle**: Heat the griddle to medium-high heat.
5. **Grill Kebabs**: Place the kebabs on the griddle and cook for 5-7 minutes per side, until the tempeh is golden and the vegetables are tender.
6. **Serve**: Serve hot with a side of rice or quinoa.

63. Grilled Chickpea Patties

Ingredients:

- 1 can chickpeas, drained and rinsed
- 1/4 cup breadcrumbs
- 1/4 cup grated carrot
- 2 tablespoons chopped fresh parsley
- 1 clove garlic, minced
- 1 teaspoon ground cumin
- 1/2 teaspoon smoked paprika
- Salt and pepper, to taste
- Olive oil for grilling

Instructions:

1. **Prepare Patties**: In a food processor, blend chickpeas, breadcrumbs, carrot, parsley, garlic, cumin, smoked paprika, salt, and pepper until well combined. Form into 4 patties.
2. **Preheat Griddle**: Heat the griddle to medium-high heat and lightly grease with olive oil.
3. **Grill Patties**: Place the patties on the griddle and cook for 4-5 minutes per side, until golden and crispy.
4. **Serve**: Serve hot on buns with your favorite toppings.

64. Grilled Seitan Cutlets

Ingredients:

- 4 seitan cutlets
- 1/4 cup olive oil
- 2 tablespoons soy sauce
- 1 tablespoon Dijon mustard

- 2 cloves garlic, minced
- 1 teaspoon dried thyme

Instructions:

1. **Prepare Marinade**: In a bowl, mix olive oil, soy sauce, Dijon mustard, garlic, and thyme.
2. **Marinate Seitan**: Place seitan cutlets in the marinade and let sit for at least 30 minutes.
3. **Preheat Griddle**: Heat the griddle to medium-high heat.
4. **Grill Seitan**: Place the seitan cutlets on the griddle and cook for 3-4 minutes per side, until heated through and slightly charred.
5. **Serve**: Serve hot with a side of vegetables or salad.

65. Grilled Black Bean Burgers

Ingredients:

- 1 can black beans, drained and rinsed
- 1/4 cup breadcrumbs
- 1/4 cup corn kernels
- 1/4 cup diced red bell pepper
- 1/4 cup chopped fresh cilantro
- 1 teaspoon ground cumin
- 1/2 teaspoon chili powder
- Salt and pepper, to taste
- Olive oil for grilling

Instructions:

1. **Prepare Patties**: In a bowl, mash black beans. Add breadcrumbs, corn, red bell pepper, cilantro, cumin, chili powder, salt, and pepper. Mix well and form into 4 patties.
2. **Preheat Griddle**: Heat the griddle to medium-high heat and lightly grease with olive oil.

3. **Grill Patties**: Place the patties on the griddle and cook for 4-5 minutes per side, until golden and crispy.

4. **Serve**: Serve hot on buns with your favorite toppings.

66. Grilled Lentil Sliders

Ingredients:

- 1 cup cooked lentils
- 1/4 cup breadcrumbs
- 1/4 cup grated carrot
- 2 tablespoons chopped fresh parsley
- 1 clove garlic, minced
- 1 teaspoon ground cumin
- 1/2 teaspoon smoked paprika
- Salt and pepper, to taste
- Olive oil for grilling
- Slider buns for serving

Instructions:

1. **Prepare Patties**: In a bowl, mix lentils, breadcrumbs, carrot, parsley, garlic, cumin, smoked paprika, salt, and pepper. Form into small slider-sized patties.

2. **Preheat Griddle**: Heat the griddle to medium-high heat and lightly grease with olive oil.

3. **Grill Patties**: Place the patties on the griddle and cook for 3-4 minutes per side, until golden and crispy.

4. **Serve**: Serve hot on slider buns with your favorite toppings.

67. Grilled Veggie Sausages

Ingredients:

- 4 veggie sausages
- 1 tablespoon olive oil
- 1 red bell pepper, sliced
- 1 yellow bell pepper, sliced
- 1 red onion, sliced
- Hot dog buns for serving

Instructions:

1. **Prepare Vegetables**: Toss bell peppers and onion slices with olive oil.
2. **Preheat Griddle**: Heat the griddle to medium-high heat.
3. **Grill Sausages and Vegetables**: Place veggie sausages and vegetables on the griddle. Cook sausages for 4-5 minutes per side, until heated through and slightly charred. Cook vegetables for 5-7 minutes, until tender and charred.
4. **Serve**: Serve grilled veggie sausages on hot dog buns with grilled vegetables on top.

68. Grilled Falafel Patties

Ingredients:

- 1 can chickpeas, drained and rinsed
- 1/4 cup chopped fresh parsley
- 1/4 cup chopped fresh cilantro
- 2 cloves garlic, minced
- 1 teaspoon ground cumin

- 1 teaspoon ground coriander
- 1/2 teaspoon baking powder
- 2 tablespoons flour
- Salt and pepper, to taste
- Olive oil for grilling

Instructions:

1. **Prepare Patties**: In a food processor, blend chickpeas, parsley, cilantro, garlic, cumin, coriander, baking powder, flour, salt, and pepper until smooth. Form into small patties.
2. **Preheat Griddle**: Heat the griddle to medium-high heat and lightly grease with olive oil.
3. **Grill Patties**: Place the patties on the griddle and cook for 3-4 minutes per side, until golden and crispy.
4. **Serve**: Serve hot in pita bread with lettuce, tomatoes, and tzatziki sauce.

69. Grilled Quinoa-Stuffed Bell Peppers

Ingredients:

- 4 bell peppers, tops cut off and seeds removed
- 1 cup cooked quinoa
- 1 can black beans, drained and rinsed
- 1 cup corn kernels
- 1 cup diced tomatoes
- 1 teaspoon ground cumin
- 1 teaspoon chili powder
- Salt and pepper, to taste
- 1/4 cup shredded cheddar cheese

Instructions:

1. **Prepare Filling**: In a bowl, mix cooked quinoa, black beans, corn, diced tomatoes, cumin, chili powder, salt, and pepper.

2. **Stuff Peppers**: Stuff each bell pepper with the quinoa mixture.

3. **Preheat Griddle**: Heat the griddle to medium-high heat.

4. **Grill Peppers**: Place the stuffed peppers on the griddle and cook for 15-20 minutes, until the peppers are tender and slightly charred.

5. **Add Cheese**: Sprinkle the tops with cheddar cheese and cook for an additional 5 minutes, until the cheese is melted.

6. **Serve**: Serve hot as a main dish.

70. Grilled Mushroom and Spinach Quesadillas

Ingredients:

- 8 large flour tortillas
- 1 cup sliced mushrooms
- 2 cups fresh spinach leaves
- 1 cup shredded mozzarella cheese
- 1/4 cup chopped green onions
- 2 tablespoons olive oil
- Salsa and sour cream for serving

Instructions:

1. **Prepare Filling**: In a pan, sauté mushrooms and spinach in olive oil until tender.

2. **Assemble Quesadillas**: On half of each tortilla, sprinkle cheese, sautéed mushrooms and spinach, and green onions. Fold the tortilla in half to cover the filling.

3. **Preheat Griddle**: Heat the griddle to medium-high heat.

4. **Grill Quesadillas**: Place the quesadillas on the griddle and cook for 2-3 minutes per side, until the cheese is melted and the tortilla is golden brown.

5. **Serve**: Cut into wedges and serve hot with salsa and sour cream.

These ten plant-based protein recipes are flavorful and satisfying, making them perfect for any meal. Enjoy these delicious and healthy dishes, whether you're a vegetarian or simply looking to incorporate more plant-based foods into your diet!

Chapter 6: Complete Meals for Every Occasion

Succulent Meats

Grilling meats to perfection can transform any meal into a feast. Here are twelve recipes for succulent meats that will impress your family and friends.

71. Classic Grilled Ribeye Steak

Ingredients:

- 4 ribeye steaks
- 2 tablespoons olive oil
- Salt and pepper, to taste
- 2 cloves garlic, minced
- 1 tablespoon fresh rosemary, chopped

Instructions:

1. **Season Steaks**: Rub the steaks with olive oil, garlic, rosemary, salt, and pepper.
2. **Preheat Griddle**: Heat the griddle to high heat.
3. **Grill Steaks**: Place the steaks on the griddle and cook for 4-5 minutes per side for medium-rare, or until desired doneness.
4. **Rest and Serve**: Let the steaks rest for 5 minutes before serving.

72. BBQ Baby Back Ribs

Ingredients:

- 2 racks baby back ribs
- 1/4 cup brown sugar
- 2 tablespoons paprika
- 1 tablespoon garlic powder
- 1 tablespoon onion powder
- Salt and pepper, to taste
- 1 cup BBQ sauce

Instructions:

1. **Prepare Ribs**: Remove the membrane from the back of the ribs. Mix brown sugar, paprika, garlic powder, onion powder, salt, and pepper. Rub this mixture over the ribs.
2. **Preheat Griddle**: Heat the griddle to medium-low heat.
3. **Grill Ribs**: Place the ribs on the griddle and cook for 1.5-2 hours, turning occasionally.
4. **Apply BBQ Sauce**: Brush with BBQ sauce during the last 15 minutes of cooking.
5. **Serve**: Serve hot with extra BBQ sauce on the side.

73. Herb-Crusted Lamb Chops

Ingredients:

- 8 lamb chops
- 2 tablespoons olive oil
- 2 cloves garlic, minced
- 1 tablespoon fresh rosemary, chopped
- 1 tablespoon fresh thyme, chopped
- Salt and pepper, to taste

Instructions:

1. **Season Lamb**: Rub the lamb chops with olive oil, garlic, rosemary, thyme, salt, and pepper.

2. **Preheat Griddle**: Heat the griddle to medium-high heat.

3. **Grill Lamb Chops**: Place the lamb chops on the griddle and cook for 3-4 minutes per side for medium-rare, or until desired doneness.

4. **Serve**: Serve hot with your favorite sides.

74. Teriyaki Grilled Pork Tenderloin

Ingredients:

- 2 pork tenderloins
- 1/2 cup teriyaki sauce
- 2 tablespoons honey
- 1 teaspoon grated ginger
- 2 cloves garlic, minced

Instructions:

1. **Marinate Pork**: In a bowl, mix teriyaki sauce, honey, ginger, and garlic. Add the pork tenderloins and marinate for at least 30 minutes.

2. **Preheat Griddle**: Heat the griddle to medium-high heat.

3. **Grill Pork**: Place the pork on the griddle and cook for 6-8 minutes per side, or until the internal temperature reaches 145°F (63°C).

4. **Rest and Serve**: Let the pork rest for 5 minutes before slicing and serving.

75. Honey Garlic Chicken Thighs

Ingredients:

- 8 boneless, skinless chicken thighs
- 1/4 cup honey
- 2 tablespoons soy sauce
- 2 cloves garlic, minced
- 1 tablespoon olive oil
- Salt and pepper, to taste

Instructions:

1. **Marinate Chicken**: In a bowl, mix honey, soy sauce, garlic, olive oil, salt, and pepper. Add the chicken thighs and marinate for at least 30 minutes.
2. **Preheat Griddle**: Heat the griddle to medium-high heat.
3. **Grill Chicken**: Place the chicken thighs on the griddle and cook for 6-7 minutes per side, or until fully cooked.
4. **Serve**: Serve hot with your favorite sides.

76. Grilled Beef Kebabs

Ingredients:

- 1 lb beef sirloin, cut into 1-inch cubes
- 1/4 cup olive oil
- 2 tablespoons soy sauce
- 1 tablespoon lemon juice
- 2 cloves garlic, minced
- Salt and pepper, to taste
- Skewers

Instructions:

1. **Marinate Beef**: In a bowl, mix olive oil, soy sauce, lemon juice, garlic, salt, and pepper. Add the beef cubes and marinate for at least 30 minutes.

2. **Preheat Griddle**: Heat the griddle to medium-high heat.

3. **Assemble Kebabs**: Thread the beef cubes onto skewers.

4. **Grill Kebabs**: Place the skewers on the griddle and cook for 4-5 minutes per side, or until desired doneness.

5. **Serve**: Serve hot with a side of rice or vegetables.

77. Spicy Grilled Sausages

Ingredients:

- 8 spicy Italian sausages
- 2 bell peppers, sliced
- 1 onion, sliced
- 1 tablespoon olive oil
- Salt and pepper, to taste

Instructions:

1. **Preheat Griddle**: Heat the griddle to medium-high heat.

2. **Grill Sausages**: Place the sausages on the griddle and cook for 8-10 minutes, turning occasionally, until fully cooked.

3. **Cook Vegetables**: In a bowl, toss bell peppers and onion with olive oil, salt, and pepper. Add to the griddle and cook until tender, about 5 minutes.

4. **Serve**: Serve sausages with grilled peppers and onions.

78. Garlic Rosemary Grilled Pork Chops

Ingredients:

- 4 bone-in pork chops
- 2 tablespoons olive oil
- 2 cloves garlic, minced
- 1 tablespoon fresh rosemary, chopped
- Salt and pepper, to taste

Instructions:

1. **Season Pork Chops**: Rub the pork chops with olive oil, garlic, rosemary, salt, and pepper.
2. **Preheat Griddle**: Heat the griddle to medium-high heat.
3. **Grill Pork Chops**: Place the pork chops on the griddle and cook for 5-6 minutes per side, or until the internal temperature reaches 145°F (63°C).
4. **Rest and Serve**: Let the pork chops rest for 5 minutes before serving.

79. Grilled Turkey Burgers

Ingredients:

- 1 lb ground turkey
- 1/4 cup breadcrumbs
- 1 egg
- 1 clove garlic, minced
- 1 teaspoon dried oregano
- Salt and pepper, to taste

- 4 hamburger buns

Instructions:

1. **Prepare Patties**: In a bowl, mix ground turkey, breadcrumbs, egg, garlic, oregano, salt, and pepper. Form into four patties.

2. **Preheat Griddle**: Heat the griddle to medium-high heat.

3. **Grill Patties**: Place the patties on the griddle and cook for 5-6 minutes per side, or until fully cooked.

4. **Toast Buns**: Toast the hamburger buns on the griddle.

5. **Assemble and Serve**: Place each patty on a bun and add your favorite toppings. Serve hot.

80. Grilled Lamb Skewers

Ingredients:

- 1 lb lamb, cut into 1-inch cubes
- 1/4 cup olive oil
- 2 cloves garlic, minced
- 1 tablespoon fresh mint, chopped
- 1 tablespoon fresh oregano, chopped
- Salt and pepper, to taste
- Skewers

Instructions:

1. **Marinate Lamb**: In a bowl, mix olive oil, garlic, mint, oregano, salt, and pepper. Add the lamb cubes and marinate for at least 30 minutes.

2. **Preheat Griddle**: Heat the griddle to medium-high heat.

3. **Assemble Skewers**: Thread the lamb cubes onto skewers.

4. **Grill Skewers**: Place the skewers on the griddle and cook for 4-5 minutes per side, or until desired doneness.

5. **Serve**: Serve hot with a side of tzatziki sauce.

81. Grilled BBQ Chicken

Ingredients:

- 4 bone-in chicken breasts
- 1/2 cup BBQ sauce
- 2 tablespoons olive oil
- Salt and pepper, to taste

Instructions:

1. **Season Chicken**: Rub the chicken breasts with olive oil, salt, and pepper.
2. **Preheat Griddle**: Heat the griddle to medium-high heat.
3. **Grill Chicken**: Place the chicken on the griddle and cook for 6-7 minutes per side, or until fully cooked.
4. **Brush with BBQ Sauce**: During the last few minutes of cooking, brush the chicken with BBQ sauce.
5. **Serve**: Serve hot with extra BBQ sauce on the side.

82. Grilled Beef Tenderloin

Ingredients:

- 4 beef tenderloin steaks
- 2 tablespoons olive oil
- 2 cloves garlic, minced
- 1 tablespoon fresh thyme, chopped
- Salt and pepper, to taste

Instructions:

1. **Season Steaks**: Rub the steaks with olive oil, garlic, thyme, salt, and pepper.

2. **Preheat Griddle**: Heat the griddle to high heat.

3. **Grill Steaks**: Place the steaks on the griddle and cook for 4-5 minutes per side for medium-rare, or until desired doneness.

4. **Rest and Serve**: Let the steaks rest for 5 minutes before serving.

These twelve succulent meat recipes are perfect for any occasion, offering a variety of flavors and techniques to create delicious, impressive meals. Enjoy experimenting with these recipes and making them your own!

Refined Seafood Dishes

Seafood dishes can be both elegant and delicious, making them perfect for any special occasion or a delightful meal at home. Here are ten refined seafood recipes to try on your gas griddle.

83. Grilled Shrimp Scampi

Ingredients:

- 1 lb large shrimp, peeled and deveined
- 1/4 cup olive oil
- 4 cloves garlic, minced
- Juice of 1 lemon
- 2 tablespoons fresh parsley, chopped
- Salt and pepper, to taste

Instructions:

1. **Marinate Shrimp**: In a bowl, mix olive oil, garlic, lemon juice, salt, and pepper. Add the shrimp and marinate for at least 15 minutes.

2. **Preheat Griddle**: Heat the griddle to medium-high heat.

3. **Grill Shrimp**: Place the shrimp on the griddle and cook for 2-3 minutes per side, or until pink and opaque.

4. **Garnish and Serve**: Sprinkle with fresh parsley and serve hot with lemon wedges.

84. Grilled Lobster Tails

Ingredients:

- 4 lobster tails
- 1/4 cup melted butter
- 2 cloves garlic, minced
- 1 tablespoon lemon juice
- Salt and pepper, to taste
- Fresh parsley, chopped, for garnish

Instructions:

1. **Prepare Lobster**: Cut the top shell of the lobster tails lengthwise to expose the meat. Mix melted butter, garlic, lemon juice, salt, and pepper.
2. **Preheat Griddle**: Heat the griddle to medium-high heat.
3. **Grill Lobster**: Brush the lobster meat with the butter mixture. Place the lobster tails meat side down on the griddle and cook for 5-6 minutes, then flip and cook for another 4-5 minutes.
4. **Garnish and Serve**: Sprinkle with fresh parsley and serve hot.

85. Grilled Scallops with Lemon Butter

Ingredients:

- 1 lb sea scallops
- 1/4 cup melted butter
- 1 tablespoon lemon juice
- 2 cloves garlic, minced
- Salt and pepper, to taste
- Fresh dill, chopped, for garnish

Instructions:

1. **Prepare Scallops**: Pat the scallops dry and season with salt and pepper. Mix melted butter, lemon juice, and garlic.

2. **Preheat Griddle**: Heat the griddle to medium-high heat.

3. **Grill Scallops**: Brush the scallops with the butter mixture and place them on the griddle. Cook for 2-3 minutes per side, or until golden brown and opaque.

4. **Garnish and Serve**: Sprinkle with fresh dill and serve hot.

86. Grilled Mahi Mahi with Pineapple Salsa

Ingredients:

- 4 mahi mahi fillets
- 2 tablespoons olive oil
- Salt and pepper, to taste
- 1 cup diced pineapple
- 1/2 cup diced red onion
- 1/2 cup diced red bell pepper
- 1 jalapeño, minced
- Juice of 1 lime
- Fresh cilantro, chopped, for garnish

Instructions:

1. **Season Mahi Mahi**: Rub the fillets with olive oil, salt, and pepper.

2. **Prepare Salsa**: In a bowl, mix pineapple, red onion, red bell pepper, jalapeño, lime juice, and cilantro.

3. **Preheat Griddle**: Heat the griddle to medium-high heat.

4. **Grill Mahi Mahi**: Place the fillets on the griddle and cook for 4-5 minutes per side, or until the fish is opaque and flakes easily with a fork.

5. **Serve**: Top the grilled mahi mahi with pineapple salsa and serve hot.

87. Grilled Swordfish Steaks

Ingredients:

- 4 swordfish steaks
- 1/4 cup olive oil
- Juice of 1 lemon
- 2 cloves garlic, minced
- 1 tablespoon fresh oregano, chopped
- Salt and pepper, to taste

Instructions:

1. **Marinate Swordfish**: In a bowl, mix olive oil, lemon juice, garlic, oregano, salt, and pepper. Add the swordfish steaks and marinate for at least 30 minutes.
2. **Preheat Griddle**: Heat the griddle to medium-high heat.
3. **Grill Swordfish**: Place the steaks on the griddle and cook for 4-5 minutes per side, or until the fish is opaque and flakes easily with a fork.
4. **Serve**: Serve hot with a side of your choice.

88. Grilled Tuna Steaks with Avocado Salsa

Ingredients:

- 4 tuna steaks
- 2 tablespoons olive oil
- 1 tablespoon soy sauce
- 1 teaspoon black pepper
- 1 avocado, diced

- 1/2 cup diced red onion
- Juice of 1 lime
- Fresh cilantro, chopped, for garnish

Instructions:

1. **Marinate Tuna**: In a bowl, mix olive oil, soy sauce, and black pepper. Add the tuna steaks and marinate for at least 15 minutes.
2. **Prepare Salsa**: In a bowl, mix avocado, red onion, lime juice, and cilantro.
3. **Preheat Griddle**: Heat the griddle to medium-high heat.
4. **Grill Tuna**: Place the steaks on the griddle and cook for 2-3 minutes per side for medium-rare, or longer if desired.
5. **Serve**: Top the grilled tuna with avocado salsa and serve hot.

89. Grilled Clams with Garlic Butter

Ingredients:

- 2 dozen clams
- 1/4 cup melted butter
- 2 cloves garlic, minced
- 1 tablespoon lemon juice
- Fresh parsley, chopped, for garnish

Instructions:

1. **Prepare Clams**: Clean the clams thoroughly.
2. **Prepare Garlic Butter**: In a bowl, mix melted butter, garlic, and lemon juice.
3. **Preheat Griddle**: Heat the griddle to medium-high heat.
4. **Grill Clams**: Place the clams on the griddle. Cook until they open, about 5-7 minutes. Discard any clams that do not open.
5. **Serve**: Drizzle with garlic butter, sprinkle with parsley, and serve hot.

90. Grilled Calamari with Lemon and Herbs

Ingredients:

- 1 lb calamari, cleaned and cut into rings
- 2 tablespoons olive oil
- Juice of 1 lemon
- 1 tablespoon fresh parsley, chopped
- 1 tablespoon fresh basil, chopped
- Salt and pepper, to taste

Instructions:

1. **Marinate Calamari**: In a bowl, mix olive oil, lemon juice, parsley, basil, salt, and pepper. Add the calamari and marinate for at least 15 minutes.
2. **Preheat Griddle**: Heat the griddle to medium-high heat.
3. **Grill Calamari**: Place the calamari on the griddle and cook for 2-3 minutes per side, or until opaque and tender.
4. **Serve**: Serve hot with lemon wedges.

91. Grilled Salmon with Dill Sauce

Ingredients:

- 4 salmon fillets
- 1/4 cup olive oil
- Juice of 1 lemon
- 1 tablespoon fresh dill, chopped
- Salt and pepper, to taste

- 1/2 cup sour cream
- 1 tablespoon Dijon mustard

Instructions:

1. **Marinate Salmon**: In a bowl, mix olive oil, lemon juice, dill, salt, and pepper. Add the salmon fillets and marinate for at least 15 minutes.
2. **Prepare Dill Sauce**: In a small bowl, mix sour cream, Dijon mustard, and additional dill.
3. **Preheat Griddle**: Heat the griddle to medium-high heat.
4. **Grill Salmon**: Place the salmon fillets on the griddle and cook for 4-5 minutes per side, or until the fish is opaque and flakes easily with a fork.
5. **Serve**: Serve hot with dill sauce on the side.

92. Grilled Tilapia with Mango Salsa

Ingredients:

- 4 tilapia fillets
- 2 tablespoons olive oil
- Salt and pepper, to taste
- 1 cup diced mango
- 1/2 cup diced red bell pepper
- 1/4 cup diced red onion
- Juice of 1 lime
- Fresh cilantro, chopped, for garnish

Instructions:

1. **Season Tilapia**: Rub the fillets with olive oil, salt, and pepper.
2. **Prepare Salsa**: In a bowl, mix mango, red bell pepper, red onion, lime juice, and cilantro.
3. **Preheat Griddle**: Heat the griddle to medium-high heat.

4. **Grill Tilapia**: Place the fillets on the griddle and cook for 3-4 minutes per side, or until the fish is opaque and flakes easily with a fork.

5. **Serve**: Top the grilled tilapia with mango salsa and serve hot.

These ten refined seafood dishes offer a variety of flavors and ingredients that will elevate your meals to the next level.

Irresistible Sides

Sides can make or break a meal. These eight irresistible side dishes are perfect complements to your main courses, adding flavor, texture, and color to your plates.

93. Garlic Parmesan Grilled Potatoes

Ingredients:

- 4 large potatoes, sliced into 1/4-inch rounds
- 1/4 cup olive oil
- 3 cloves garlic, minced
- 1/4 cup grated Parmesan cheese
- 1 tablespoon fresh parsley, chopped
- Salt and pepper, to taste

Instructions:

1. **Prepare Potatoes**: In a bowl, toss the potato slices with olive oil, garlic, salt, and pepper.
2. **Preheat Griddle**: Heat the griddle to medium-high heat.
3. **Grill Potatoes**: Place the potato slices on the griddle and cook for 5-7 minutes per side, or until tender and golden brown.
4. **Add Parmesan and Parsley**: Sprinkle with Parmesan cheese and fresh parsley.
5. **Serve**: Serve hot as a side dish.

94. Grilled Asparagus with Lemon Zest

Ingredients:

- 1 bunch asparagus, trimmed
- 2 tablespoons olive oil
- Zest of 1 lemon
- Salt and pepper, to taste
- Lemon wedges for serving

Instructions:

1. **Prepare Asparagus**: In a bowl, toss the asparagus with olive oil, lemon zest, salt, and pepper.
2. **Preheat Griddle**: Heat the griddle to medium-high heat.
3. **Grill Asparagus**: Place the asparagus on the griddle and cook for 4-5 minutes, turning occasionally, until tender and slightly charred.
4. **Serve**: Serve hot with lemon wedges.

95. Grilled Corn on the Cob with Chili Lime Butter

Ingredients:

- 4 ears of corn, husked
- 1/4 cup butter, melted
- 1 teaspoon chili powder
- Zest and juice of 1 lime
- Salt, to taste
- Fresh cilantro, chopped, for garnish

Instructions:

1. **Prepare Butter**: In a bowl, mix melted butter, chili powder, lime zest, lime juice, and salt.

2. **Preheat Griddle**: Heat the griddle to medium-high heat.

3. **Grill Corn**: Place the corn on the griddle and cook for 10-12 minutes, turning occasionally, until the corn is tender and slightly charred.

4. **Add Butter**: Brush the chili lime butter over the grilled corn.

5. **Garnish and Serve**: Sprinkle with fresh cilantro and serve hot.

96. Grilled Brussels Sprouts with Balsamic Glaze

Ingredients:

- 1 lb Brussels sprouts, halved
- 2 tablespoons olive oil
- Salt and pepper, to taste
- 1/4 cup balsamic glaze

Instructions:

1. **Prepare Brussels Sprouts**: In a bowl, toss the Brussels sprouts with olive oil, salt, and pepper.

2. **Preheat Griddle**: Heat the griddle to medium-high heat.

3. **Grill Brussels Sprouts**: Place the Brussels sprouts on the griddle and cook for 6-8 minutes, turning occasionally, until tender and charred.

4. **Add Balsamic Glaze**: Drizzle with balsamic glaze.

5. **Serve**: Serve hot as a side dish.

97. Grilled Sweet Potato Wedges

Ingredients:

- 2 large sweet potatoes, cut into wedges
- 2 tablespoons olive oil
- 1 teaspoon smoked paprika

- Salt and pepper, to taste
- Fresh parsley, chopped, for garnish

Instructions:

1. **Prepare Sweet Potatoes**: In a bowl, toss the sweet potato wedges with olive oil, smoked paprika, salt, and pepper.
2. **Preheat Griddle**: Heat the griddle to medium-high heat.
3. **Grill Sweet Potatoes**: Place the sweet potato wedges on the griddle and cook for 5-7 minutes per side, or until tender and charred.
4. **Garnish and Serve**: Sprinkle with fresh parsley and serve hot.

98. Grilled Zucchini and Squash

Ingredients:

- 2 zucchinis, sliced lengthwise
- 2 yellow squashes, sliced lengthwise
- 2 tablespoons olive oil
- 1 teaspoon Italian seasoning
- Salt and pepper, to taste

Instructions:

1. **Prepare Vegetables**: In a bowl, toss the zucchini and squash slices with olive oil, Italian seasoning, salt, and pepper.
2. **Preheat Griddle**: Heat the griddle to medium-high heat.
3. **Grill Vegetables**: Place the zucchini and squash on the griddle and cook for 4-5 minutes per side, or until tender and charred.
4. **Serve**: Serve hot as a side dish.

99. Grilled Mushrooms with Thyme

Ingredients:

- 1 lb mixed mushrooms (such as cremini, portobello, and shiitake), cleaned and sliced
- 2 tablespoons olive oil
- 1 tablespoon fresh thyme, chopped
- 2 cloves garlic, minced
- Salt and pepper, to taste

Instructions:

1. **Prepare Mushrooms**: In a bowl, toss the mushrooms with olive oil, thyme, garlic, salt, and pepper.
2. **Preheat Griddle**: Heat the griddle to medium-high heat.
3. **Grill Mushrooms**: Place the mushrooms on the griddle and cook for 5-7 minutes, stirring occasionally, until tender and golden brown.
4. **Serve**: Serve hot as a side dish.

100. Grilled Eggplant with Mint Yogurt Sauce

Ingredients:

- 2 large eggplants, sliced into rounds
- 2 tablespoons olive oil
- Salt and pepper, to taste
- 1 cup plain Greek yogurt
- 1 tablespoon fresh mint, chopped
- 1 clove garlic, minced
- Juice of 1 lemon

Instructions:

1. **Prepare Eggplant**: In a bowl, toss the eggplant slices with olive oil, salt, and pepper.
2. **Prepare Sauce**: In a small bowl, mix Greek yogurt, mint, garlic, lemon juice, salt, and pepper.
3. **Preheat Griddle**: Heat the griddle to medium-high heat.
4. **Grill Eggplant**: Place the eggplant slices on the griddle and cook for 4-5 minutes per side, or until tender and charred.
5. **Serve**: Serve hot with mint yogurt sauce on the side.

These eight irresistible side dishes are perfect complements to any meal, adding flavor, texture, and variety to your plate. Enjoy experimenting with these recipes and making them your own!

Chapter 7: International Cuisine on the Grill

Mexican Recipes

Bring the vibrant flavors of Mexico to your grill with these eight delicious recipes. From tacos to grilled corn, these dishes are sure to add a spicy kick to your meals.

101. Grilled Chicken Tacos

Ingredients:

- 4 boneless, skinless chicken breasts
- 2 tablespoons olive oil
- 1 tablespoon chili powder
- 1 teaspoon cumin
- 1 teaspoon garlic powder
- Salt and pepper, to taste
- 8 small flour or corn tortillas
- 1 cup diced tomatoes
- 1 cup shredded lettuce
- 1/2 cup chopped cilantro

- Lime wedges for serving

Instructions:

1. **Marinate Chicken**: In a bowl, mix olive oil, chili powder, cumin, garlic powder, salt, and pepper. Add the chicken breasts and marinate for at least 30 minutes.

2. **Preheat Griddle**: Heat the griddle to medium-high heat.

3. **Grill Chicken**: Place the chicken on the griddle and cook for 6-7 minutes per side, or until fully cooked. Remove and let rest for 5 minutes, then slice.

4. **Warm Tortillas**: Warm the tortillas on the griddle for 1-2 minutes per side.

5. **Assemble Tacos**: Fill each tortilla with grilled chicken, diced tomatoes, shredded lettuce, and cilantro.

6. **Serve**: Serve hot with lime wedges.

102. Carne Asada

Ingredients:

- 1 1/2 lbs flank steak
- 1/4 cup olive oil
- 1/4 cup lime juice
- 2 cloves garlic, minced
- 1 teaspoon ground cumin
- 1 teaspoon chili powder
- 1 teaspoon oregano
- Salt and pepper, to taste
- Sliced onions and jalapeños for garnish

Instructions:

1. **Marinate Steak**: In a bowl, mix olive oil, lime juice, garlic, cumin, chili powder, oregano, salt, and pepper. Add the flank steak and marinate for at least 2 hours.
2. **Preheat Griddle**: Heat the griddle to high heat.
3. **Grill Steak**: Place the steak on the griddle and cook for 5-6 minutes per side, or until desired doneness.
4. **Rest and Slice**: Let the steak rest for 5 minutes before slicing thinly against the grain.
5. **Serve**: Serve hot with sliced onions and jalapeños.

103. Grilled Fish Tacos

Ingredients:

- 1 lb white fish fillets (such as cod or tilapia)
- 2 tablespoons olive oil
- 1 teaspoon chili powder
- 1 teaspoon cumin
- 1/2 teaspoon paprika
- Salt and pepper, to taste
- 8 small flour or corn tortillas
- 1 cup shredded cabbage
- 1/2 cup diced tomatoes
- 1/4 cup chopped cilantro
- Lime wedges for serving

Instructions:

1. **Season Fish**: Rub the fish fillets with olive oil, chili powder, cumin, paprika, salt, and pepper.
2. **Preheat Griddle**: Heat the griddle to medium-high heat.

3. **Grill Fish**: Place the fish on the griddle and cook for 3-4 minutes per side, or until the fish is opaque and flakes easily.

4. **Warm Tortillas**: Warm the tortillas on the griddle for 1-2 minutes per side.

5. **Assemble Tacos**: Fill each tortilla with grilled fish, shredded cabbage, diced tomatoes, and cilantro.

6. **Serve**: Serve hot with lime wedges.

104. Grilled Street Corn (Elote)

Ingredients:

- 4 ears of corn, husked
- 1/4 cup mayonnaise
- 1/4 cup sour cream
- 1/2 cup cotija cheese, crumbled
- 1 teaspoon chili powder
- 1 lime, cut into wedges
- Fresh cilantro, chopped, for garnish

Instructions:

1. **Preheat Griddle**: Heat the griddle to medium-high heat.

2. **Grill Corn**: Place the corn on the griddle and cook for 10-12 minutes, turning occasionally, until tender and slightly charred.

3. **Prepare Topping**: In a bowl, mix mayonnaise and sour cream. Brush the mixture over the grilled corn.

4. **Add Cheese and Spices**: Sprinkle with cotija cheese and chili powder.

5. **Garnish and Serve**: Serve hot with lime wedges and fresh cilantro.

105. Grilled Shrimp Fajitas

Ingredients:

- 1 lb large shrimp, peeled and deveined
- 2 bell peppers, sliced
- 1 large onion, sliced
- 2 tablespoons olive oil
- 1 tablespoon fajita seasoning
- 8 small flour or corn tortillas
- Lime wedges for serving

Instructions:

1. **Prepare Shrimp and Vegetables**: In a bowl, toss the shrimp, bell peppers, and onion with olive oil and fajita seasoning.
2. **Preheat Griddle**: Heat the griddle to medium-high heat.
3. **Grill Shrimp and Vegetables**: Place the shrimp and vegetables on the griddle and cook for 5-7 minutes, turning occasionally, until the shrimp are pink and the vegetables are tender.
4. **Warm Tortillas**: Warm the tortillas on the griddle for 1-2 minutes per side.
5. **Assemble Fajitas**: Fill each tortilla with grilled shrimp and vegetables.
6. **Serve**: Serve hot with lime wedges.

106. Grilled Quesadillas

Ingredients:

- 4 large flour tortillas
- 2 cups shredded cheese (cheddar, Monterey Jack, or a blend)
- 1 cup cooked and shredded chicken or beef
- 1/2 cup diced tomatoes

- 1/4 cup chopped cilantro
- Sour cream and salsa for serving

Instructions:

1. **Assemble Quesadillas**: On one half of each tortilla, sprinkle cheese, cooked meat, tomatoes, and cilantro. Fold the tortilla in half to cover the filling.
2. **Preheat Griddle**: Heat the griddle to medium-high heat.
3. **Grill Quesadillas**: Place the quesadillas on the griddle and cook for 2-3 minutes per side, or until the cheese is melted and the tortillas are golden brown.
4. **Serve**: Cut into wedges and serve hot with sour cream and salsa.

107. Grilled Mexican Street Tacos

Ingredients:

- 1 lb skirt steak or flank steak
- 1/4 cup olive oil
- 1/4 cup lime juice
- 2 cloves garlic, minced
- 1 teaspoon ground cumin
- 1 teaspoon chili powder
- Salt and pepper, to taste
- 8 small flour or corn tortillas
- 1/2 cup diced onions
- 1/4 cup chopped cilantro
- Lime wedges for serving

Instructions:

1. **Marinate Steak**: In a bowl, mix olive oil, lime juice, garlic, cumin, chili powder, salt, and pepper. Add the steak and marinate for at least 1 hour.

2. **Preheat Griddle**: Heat the griddle to high heat.
3. **Grill Steak**: Place the steak on the griddle and cook for 4-5 minutes per side, or until desired doneness.
4. **Rest and Slice**: Let the steak rest for 5 minutes before slicing thinly against the grain.
5. **Warm Tortillas**: Warm the tortillas on the griddle for 1-2 minutes per side.
6. **Assemble Tacos**: Fill each tortilla with grilled steak, diced onions, and cilantro.
7. **Serve**: Serve hot with lime wedges.

108. Grilled Jalapeño Poppers

Ingredients:

- 12 large jalapeños, halved and seeded
- 8 ounces cream cheese, softened
- 1/2 cup shredded cheddar cheese
- 1/4 cup cooked bacon, crumbled
- 1 tablespoon chopped chives

Instructions:

1. **Prepare Filling**: In a bowl, mix cream cheese, cheddar cheese, bacon, and chives.
2. **Fill Jalapeños**: Spoon the cream cheese mixture into each jalapeño half.
3. **Preheat Griddle**: Heat the griddle to medium-high heat.
4. **Grill Jalapeños**: Place the jalapeño poppers on the griddle, filling side up, and cook for 5-7 minutes, or until the jalapeños are tender and the filling is bubbly.
5. **Serve**: Serve hot as an appetizer or side dish.

These eight Mexican recipes are bursting with flavor and perfect for grilling. Enjoy the vibrant, spicy tastes of Mexico in your own backyard!

Italian Recipes

Bring the authentic flavors of Italy to your grill with these eight delicious recipes. From grilled pizzas to savory meats, these dishes will transport your taste buds straight to Italy.

109. Grilled Margherita Pizza

Ingredients:

- 1 lb pizza dough
- 1 cup marinara sauce
- 8 ounces fresh mozzarella, sliced
- 1/4 cup fresh basil leaves
- 2 tablespoons olive oil
- Salt and pepper, to taste

Instructions:

1. **Prepare Dough**: Roll out the pizza dough on a lightly floured surface.
2. **Preheat Griddle**: Heat the griddle to medium-high heat and brush with olive oil.
3. **Grill Dough**: Place the dough on the griddle and cook for 2-3 minutes per side, or until lightly browned and firm.
4. **Add Toppings**: Spread marinara sauce over the grilled dough, top with mozzarella slices, salt, and pepper.
5. **Finish Cooking**: Cover the griddle with a lid and cook for another 3-4 minutes, or until the cheese is melted.
6. **Garnish and Serve**: Remove from the griddle, top with fresh basil leaves, and serve hot.

110. Grilled Chicken Alfredo

Ingredients:

- 4 boneless, skinless chicken breasts
- 2 tablespoons olive oil
- 1 teaspoon Italian seasoning
- Salt and pepper, to taste
- 1 cup Alfredo sauce
- Fresh parsley, chopped, for garnish

Instructions:

1. **Season Chicken**: Rub the chicken breasts with olive oil, Italian seasoning, salt, and pepper.
2. **Preheat Griddle**: Heat the griddle to medium-high heat.
3. **Grill Chicken**: Place the chicken on the griddle and cook for 6-7 minutes per side, or until fully cooked.
4. **Heat Alfredo Sauce**: In a small saucepan, warm the Alfredo sauce on the griddle.
5. **Serve**: Slice the grilled chicken and serve with Alfredo sauce drizzled on top, garnished with fresh parsley.

111. Grilled Caprese Salad

Ingredients:

- 4 large tomatoes, sliced
- 8 ounces fresh mozzarella, sliced
- 1/4 cup fresh basil leaves
- 2 tablespoons olive oil

- Balsamic glaze, for drizzling
- Salt and pepper, to taste

Instructions:

1. **Preheat Griddle**: Heat the griddle to medium-high heat and lightly grease with olive oil.
2. **Grill Tomatoes**: Place the tomato slices on the griddle and cook for 2-3 minutes per side, until lightly charred.
3. **Assemble Salad**: Arrange grilled tomatoes and mozzarella slices on a serving platter. Top with fresh basil leaves.
4. **Season and Serve**: Drizzle with olive oil and balsamic glaze, sprinkle with salt and pepper, and serve.

112. Grilled Italian Sausage and Peppers

Ingredients:

- 4 Italian sausages
- 2 bell peppers (red and yellow), sliced
- 1 large onion, sliced
- 2 tablespoons olive oil
- 1 teaspoon Italian seasoning
- Salt and pepper, to taste

Instructions:

1. **Prepare Vegetables**: In a bowl, toss bell peppers and onion with olive oil, Italian seasoning, salt, and pepper.
2. **Preheat Griddle**: Heat the griddle to medium-high heat.
3. **Grill Sausages**: Place the sausages on the griddle and cook for 10-12 minutes, turning occasionally, until fully cooked.
4. **Grill Vegetables**: Add the bell peppers and onion to the griddle and cook for 5-7 minutes, until tender and slightly charred.

5. **Serve**: Serve the grilled sausages with the peppers and onions.

113. Grilled Eggplant Parmesan

Ingredients:

- 2 large eggplants, sliced into rounds
- 1/4 cup olive oil
- 1 cup marinara sauce
- 1 cup shredded mozzarella cheese
- 1/2 cup grated Parmesan cheese
- Fresh basil leaves, for garnish
- Salt and pepper, to taste

Instructions:

1. **Prepare Eggplant**: Brush eggplant slices with olive oil and season with salt and pepper.
2. **Preheat Griddle**: Heat the griddle to medium-high heat.
3. **Grill Eggplant**: Place the eggplant slices on the griddle and cook for 3-4 minutes per side, until tender and lightly charred.
4. **Assemble Parmesan**: Place grilled eggplant slices on a baking sheet. Top with marinara sauce, mozzarella cheese, and Parmesan cheese.
5. **Melt Cheese**: Place the baking sheet under a broiler for 3-4 minutes, until the cheese is melted and bubbly.
6. **Garnish and Serve**: Garnish with fresh basil leaves and serve hot.

114. Grilled Bruschetta

Ingredients:

- 1 baguette, sliced
- 4 large tomatoes, diced
- 2 cloves garlic, minced
- 1/4 cup fresh basil, chopped
- 2 tablespoons olive oil
- Balsamic vinegar, for drizzling
- Salt and pepper, to taste

Instructions:

1. **Prepare Topping**: In a bowl, mix diced tomatoes, garlic, basil, olive oil, salt, and pepper.
2. **Preheat Griddle**: Heat the griddle to medium-high heat.
3. **Grill Bread**: Brush baguette slices with olive oil and place on the griddle. Grill for 2-3 minutes per side, until toasted.
4. **Assemble Bruschetta**: Spoon the tomato mixture onto the grilled bread slices.
5. **Serve**: Drizzle with balsamic vinegar and serve immediately.

115. Grilled Prosciutto-Wrapped Asparagus

Ingredients:

- 1 bunch asparagus, trimmed
- 8 slices prosciutto
- 2 tablespoons olive oil
- Salt and pepper, to taste

Instructions:

1. **Wrap Asparagus**: Wrap each asparagus spear with a slice of prosciutto.
2. **Preheat Griddle**: Heat the griddle to medium-high heat.
3. **Grill Asparagus**: Drizzle the wrapped asparagus with olive oil and season with salt and pepper. Place on the griddle and cook for 4-5 minutes, turning occasionally, until the prosciutto is crispy and the asparagus is tender.
4. **Serve**: Serve hot as an appetizer or side dish.

116. Grilled Balsamic Chicken

Ingredients:

- 4 boneless, skinless chicken breasts
- 1/4 cup balsamic vinegar
- 2 tablespoons olive oil
- 2 cloves garlic, minced
- 1 teaspoon dried basil
- Salt and pepper, to taste
- Fresh basil leaves for garnish

Instructions:

1. **Marinate Chicken**: In a bowl, mix balsamic vinegar, olive oil, garlic, dried basil, salt, and pepper. Add the chicken breasts and marinate for at least 30 minutes.
2. **Preheat Griddle**: Heat the griddle to medium-high heat.
3. **Grill Chicken**: Place the chicken on the griddle and cook for 6-7 minutes per side, or until fully cooked.
4. **Serve**: Garnish with fresh basil leaves and serve hot.

These eight Italian recipes are perfect for grilling, offering a variety of flavors and ingredients that will delight your taste buds and transport you to Italy. Enjoy these dishes with friends and family for a true Italian dining experience!

Asian Recipes

Experience the diverse and vibrant flavors of Asia with these eight delicious recipes. From savory skewers to flavorful marinades, these dishes are perfect for grilling and will add an exotic touch to your meals.

117. Grilled Teriyaki Chicken Skewers

Ingredients:

- 1 lb boneless, skinless chicken thighs, cut into 1-inch pieces
- 1/2 cup teriyaki sauce
- 2 tablespoons soy sauce
- 1 tablespoon honey
- 1 tablespoon sesame oil
- 1 tablespoon sesame seeds
- 2 green onions, chopped
- Skewers

Instructions:

1. **Marinate Chicken**: In a bowl, mix teriyaki sauce, soy sauce, honey, and sesame oil. Add the chicken pieces and marinate for at least 30 minutes.
2. **Preheat Griddle**: Heat the griddle to medium-high heat.
3. **Assemble Skewers**: Thread the marinated chicken onto skewers.
4. **Grill Skewers**: Place the skewers on the griddle and cook for 5-7 minutes per side, or until the chicken is fully cooked and caramelized.
5. **Garnish and Serve**: Sprinkle with sesame seeds and chopped green onions. Serve hot.

118. Grilled Miso Salmon

Ingredients:

- 4 salmon fillets
- 1/4 cup miso paste
- 2 tablespoons soy sauce
- 2 tablespoons sake (optional)
- 1 tablespoon sugar
- 1 tablespoon sesame oil
- Lemon wedges for serving

Instructions:

1. **Marinate Salmon**: In a bowl, mix miso paste, soy sauce, sake, sugar, and sesame oil. Add the salmon fillets and marinate for at least 30 minutes.
2. **Preheat Griddle**: Heat the griddle to medium-high heat.
3. **Grill Salmon**: Place the salmon fillets on the griddle and cook for 4-5 minutes per side, or until the fish is opaque and flakes easily with a fork.
4. **Serve**: Serve hot with lemon wedges.

119. Grilled Thai Beef Salad

Ingredients:

- 1 lb flank steak
- 2 tablespoons soy sauce
- 1 tablespoon fish sauce
- 1 tablespoon lime juice
- 1 teaspoon sugar
- 1 clove garlic, minced

- 1 red chili, thinly sliced
- 4 cups mixed salad greens
- 1/2 cup cherry tomatoes, halved
- 1/4 cup fresh mint leaves
- 1/4 cup fresh cilantro leaves
- 1/4 cup chopped peanuts

Instructions:

1. **Marinate Steak**: In a bowl, mix soy sauce, fish sauce, lime juice, sugar, garlic, and chili. Add the flank steak and marinate for at least 1 hour.
2. **Preheat Griddle**: Heat the griddle to high heat.
3. **Grill Steak**: Place the steak on the griddle and cook for 5-6 minutes per side, or until desired doneness. Let rest for 5 minutes before slicing thinly.
4. **Assemble Salad**: In a large bowl, combine salad greens, cherry tomatoes, mint, cilantro, and chopped peanuts.
5. **Serve**: Top the salad with sliced steak and serve with additional dressing if desired.

120. Grilled Soy-Ginger Shrimp

Ingredients:

- 1 lb large shrimp, peeled and deveined
- 1/4 cup soy sauce
- 2 tablespoons honey
- 1 tablespoon rice vinegar
- 1 tablespoon grated ginger
- 2 cloves garlic, minced
- 1 tablespoon sesame oil
- Skewers

Instructions:

1. **Marinate Shrimp**: In a bowl, mix soy sauce, honey, rice vinegar, ginger, garlic, and sesame oil. Add the shrimp and marinate for at least 15 minutes.

2. **Preheat Griddle**: Heat the griddle to medium-high heat.

3. **Assemble Skewers**: Thread the shrimp onto skewers.

4. **Grill Shrimp**: Place the skewers on the griddle and cook for 2-3 minutes per side, or until the shrimp are pink and opaque.

5. **Serve**: Serve hot as an appetizer or main dish.

121. Grilled Korean BBQ Short Ribs (Galbi)

Ingredients:

- 2 lbs Korean-style short ribs
- 1/2 cup soy sauce
- 1/4 cup brown sugar
- 2 tablespoons sesame oil
- 2 tablespoons rice vinegar
- 4 cloves garlic, minced
- 1 tablespoon grated ginger
- 1 pear, grated
- 1/4 cup chopped green onions
- Sesame seeds for garnish

Instructions:

1. **Marinate Ribs**: In a bowl, mix soy sauce, brown sugar, sesame oil, rice vinegar, garlic, ginger, and grated pear. Add the short ribs and marinate for at least 2 hours.

2. **Preheat Griddle**: Heat the griddle to medium-high heat.

3. **Grill Ribs**: Place the short ribs on the griddle and cook for 3-4 minutes per side, or until the meat is caramelized and cooked through.

4. **Garnish and Serve**: Sprinkle with chopped green onions and sesame seeds. Serve hot.

122. Grilled Tandoori Chicken

Ingredients:

- 4 boneless, skinless chicken breasts
- 1 cup plain yogurt
- 2 tablespoons lemon juice
- 2 cloves garlic, minced
- 1 tablespoon grated ginger
- 2 teaspoons ground cumin
- 2 teaspoons ground coriander
- 1 teaspoon ground turmeric
- 1 teaspoon chili powder
- Salt and pepper, to taste
- Fresh cilantro, chopped, for garnish

Instructions:

1. **Marinate Chicken**: In a bowl, mix yogurt, lemon juice, garlic, ginger, cumin, coriander, turmeric, chili powder, salt, and pepper. Add the chicken breasts and marinate for at least 1 hour.

2. **Preheat Griddle**: Heat the griddle to medium-high heat.

3. **Grill Chicken**: Place the chicken on the griddle and cook for 6-7 minutes per side, or until fully cooked.

4. **Garnish and Serve**: Garnish with fresh cilantro and serve hot with naan bread or rice.

123. Grilled Teriyaki Pineapple Pork Chops

Ingredients:

- 4 boneless pork chops
- 1/2 cup teriyaki sauce
- 1/4 cup pineapple juice
- 1 tablespoon brown sugar
- 2 cloves garlic, minced
- 1 teaspoon grated ginger
- 4 pineapple rings

Instructions:

1. **Marinate Pork Chops**: In a bowl, mix teriyaki sauce, pineapple juice, brown sugar, garlic, and ginger. Add the pork chops and marinate for at least 30 minutes.
2. **Preheat Griddle**: Heat the griddle to medium-high heat.
3. **Grill Pork Chops**: Place the pork chops on the griddle and cook for 4-5 minutes per side, or until fully cooked. Grill the pineapple rings for 2-3 minutes per side.
4. **Serve**: Serve the pork chops hot with grilled pineapple rings on top.

124. Grilled Vietnamese Pork Banh Mi

Ingredients:

- 1 lb pork tenderloin, thinly sliced
- 1/4 cup soy sauce
- 2 tablespoons fish sauce
- 2 tablespoons sugar
- 2 cloves garlic, minced
- 1 tablespoon sesame oil

- 4 baguettes, split
- Pickled carrots and daikon
- Fresh cilantro
- Sliced jalapeños
- Mayonnaise

Instructions:

1. **Marinate Pork**: In a bowl, mix soy sauce, fish sauce, sugar, garlic, and sesame oil. Add the pork slices and marinate for at least 30 minutes.
2. **Preheat Griddle**: Heat the griddle to medium-high heat.
3. **Grill Pork**: Place the pork slices on the griddle and cook for 3-4 minutes per side, or until fully cooked.
4. **Assemble Banh Mi**: Spread mayonnaise on the inside of each baguette. Fill with grilled pork, pickled carrots and daikon, fresh cilantro, and sliced jalapeños.
5. **Serve**: Serve the banh mi sandwiches hot.

These eight Asian recipes offer a variety of flavors and ingredients that are perfect for grilling. Enjoy the rich and diverse tastes of Asia in your own backyard!

Fusion and Innovation

Fusion cuisine combines elements from different culinary traditions to create innovative and exciting dishes. Here are six fusion recipes that blend flavors and techniques from around the world, perfect for grilling.

125. Korean BBQ Tacos

Ingredients:

- 1 lb thinly sliced beef (such as ribeye or sirloin)
- 1/4 cup soy sauce
- 2 tablespoons brown sugar

- 2 tablespoons sesame oil
- 2 cloves garlic, minced
- 1 tablespoon grated ginger
- 1 teaspoon gochujang (Korean chili paste)
- 8 small flour or corn tortillas
- 1 cup kimchi, chopped
- 1/4 cup chopped green onions
- Sesame seeds for garnish

Instructions:

1. **Marinate Beef**: In a bowl, mix soy sauce, brown sugar, sesame oil, garlic, ginger, and gochujang. Add the beef slices and marinate for at least 30 minutes.
2. **Preheat Griddle**: Heat the griddle to medium-high heat.
3. **Grill Beef**: Place the beef on the griddle and cook for 2-3 minutes per side, or until cooked through.
4. **Warm Tortillas**: Warm the tortillas on the griddle for 1-2 minutes per side.
5. **Assemble Tacos**: Fill each tortilla with grilled beef, chopped kimchi, and green onions.
6. **Garnish and Serve**: Sprinkle with sesame seeds and serve hot.

126. Teriyaki Chicken Quesadillas

Ingredients:

- 2 boneless, skinless chicken breasts
- 1/4 cup teriyaki sauce
- 4 large flour tortillas
- 1 cup shredded Monterey Jack cheese
- 1/4 cup sliced green onions
- 2 tablespoons sesame seeds

- 1 tablespoon sesame oil
- Soy sauce for dipping

Instructions:

1. **Marinate Chicken**: In a bowl, marinate the chicken breasts in teriyaki sauce for at least 30 minutes.
2. **Preheat Griddle**: Heat the griddle to medium-high heat.
3. **Grill Chicken**: Place the chicken on the griddle and cook for 6-7 minutes per side, or until fully cooked. Slice thinly.
4. **Assemble Quesadillas**: On half of each tortilla, sprinkle cheese, grilled chicken slices, green onions, and sesame seeds. Fold the tortilla in half to cover the filling.
5. **Grill Quesadillas**: Place the quesadillas on the griddle and cook for 2-3 minutes per side, or until the cheese is melted and the tortilla is golden brown.
6. **Serve**: Cut into wedges and serve with soy sauce for dipping.

127. Mediterranean BBQ Pizza

Ingredients:

- 1 lb pizza dough
- 1/2 cup hummus
- 1/2 cup shredded mozzarella cheese
- 1/4 cup sliced black olives
- 1/4 cup diced red onion
- 1/4 cup chopped sun-dried tomatoes
- 1/4 cup crumbled feta cheese
- 2 tablespoons olive oil
- Fresh basil leaves for garnish

Instructions:

1. **Prepare Dough**: Roll out the pizza dough on a lightly floured surface.
2. **Preheat Griddle**: Heat the griddle to medium-high heat and brush with olive oil.
3. **Grill Dough**: Place the dough on the griddle and cook for 2-3 minutes per side, or until lightly browned and firm.
4. **Add Toppings**: Spread hummus over the grilled dough, top with mozzarella cheese, olives, red onion, sun-dried tomatoes, and feta cheese.
5. **Finish Cooking**: Cover the griddle with a lid and cook for another 3-4 minutes, or until the cheese is melted.
6. **Garnish and Serve**: Remove from the griddle, top with fresh basil leaves, and serve hot.

128. Thai Peanut Chicken Skewers

Ingredients:

- 1 lb boneless, skinless chicken thighs, cut into 1-inch pieces
- 1/4 cup peanut butter
- 2 tablespoons soy sauce
- 2 tablespoons lime juice
- 1 tablespoon honey
- 1 tablespoon grated ginger
- 2 cloves garlic, minced
- 1/4 cup chopped cilantro
- Skewers

Instructions:

1. **Prepare Marinade**: In a bowl, mix peanut butter, soy sauce, lime juice, honey, ginger, and garlic. Add the chicken pieces and marinate for at least 30 minutes.
2. **Preheat Griddle**: Heat the griddle to medium-high heat.

3. **Assemble Skewers**: Thread the marinated chicken onto skewers.
4. **Grill Skewers**: Place the skewers on the griddle and cook for 5-7 minutes per side, or until the chicken is fully cooked and slightly charred.
5. **Garnish and Serve**: Sprinkle with chopped cilantro and serve hot.

129. BBQ Pork Banh Mi Sandwich

Ingredients:

- 1 lb pork tenderloin, thinly sliced
- 1/4 cup BBQ sauce
- 1 tablespoon soy sauce
- 1 tablespoon honey
- 4 baguettes, split
- Pickled carrots and daikon
- Fresh cilantro
- Sliced jalapeños
- Mayonnaise

Instructions:

1. **Marinate Pork**: In a bowl, mix BBQ sauce, soy sauce, and honey. Add the pork slices and marinate for at least 30 minutes.
2. **Preheat Griddle**: Heat the griddle to medium-high heat.
3. **Grill Pork**: Place the pork slices on the griddle and cook for 3-4 minutes per side, or until fully cooked.
4. **Assemble Sandwiches**: Spread mayonnaise on the inside of each baguette. Fill with grilled pork, pickled carrots and daikon, fresh cilantro, and sliced jalapeños.
5. **Serve**: Serve the banh mi sandwiches hot.

130. Spicy Tandoori Fish Tacos

Ingredients:

- 1 lb white fish fillets (such as cod or tilapia)
- 1/2 cup plain yogurt
- 1 tablespoon lemon juice
- 2 cloves garlic, minced
- 1 tablespoon grated ginger
- 1 teaspoon ground cumin
- 1 teaspoon ground coriander
- 1 teaspoon ground turmeric
- 1 teaspoon chili powder
- 8 small flour or corn tortillas
- 1 cup shredded lettuce
- 1/2 cup diced tomatoes
- 1/4 cup chopped cilantro
- Lime wedges for serving

Instructions:

1. **Prepare Marinade**: In a bowl, mix yogurt, lemon juice, garlic, ginger, cumin, coriander, turmeric, and chili powder. Add the fish fillets and marinate for at least 30 minutes.
2. **Preheat Griddle**: Heat the griddle to medium-high heat.
3. **Grill Fish**: Place the fish on the griddle and cook for 3-4 minutes per side, or until the fish is opaque and flakes easily.
4. **Warm Tortillas**: Warm the tortillas on the griddle for 1-2 minutes per side.

5. **Assemble Tacos**: Fill each tortilla with grilled fish, shredded lettuce, diced tomatoes, and cilantro.

6. **Serve**: Serve hot with lime wedges.

These six fusion recipes combine flavors and techniques from different culinary traditions, creating innovative and delicious dishes perfect for grilling. Enjoy these unique and exciting meals with friends and family!

Chapter 8: Grilled Desserts

Grilled Fruits and Desserts

Grilling isn't just for savory dishes – it can also bring out the natural sweetness in fruits and create delicious desserts with a smoky, caramelized touch. Here are six recipes for grilled fruits and desserts that will satisfy your sweet tooth.

131. Grilled Pineapple with Cinnamon Sugar

Ingredients:

- 1 pineapple, peeled, cored, and cut into rings
- 2 tablespoons melted butter
- 2 tablespoons brown sugar
- 1 teaspoon ground cinnamon

Instructions:

1. **Prepare Pineapple**: Brush the pineapple rings with melted butter.
2. **Mix Sugar and Cinnamon**: In a small bowl, mix brown sugar and cinnamon. Sprinkle over both sides of the pineapple rings.
3. **Preheat Griddle**: Heat the griddle to medium-high heat.
4. **Grill Pineapple**: Place the pineapple rings on the griddle and cook for 2-3 minutes per side, or until caramelized and slightly charred.
5. **Serve**: Serve hot with a scoop of vanilla ice cream.

132. Grilled Peaches with Honey and Mascarpone

Ingredients:

- 4 ripe peaches, halved and pitted
- 2 tablespoons olive oil
- 1/4 cup honey
- 1/2 cup mascarpone cheese
- Fresh mint leaves for garnish

Instructions:

1. **Prepare Peaches**: Brush the peach halves with olive oil.
2. **Preheat Griddle**: Heat the griddle to medium-high heat.
3. **Grill Peaches**: Place the peaches cut side down on the griddle and cook for 3-4 minutes, or until tender and caramelized.
4. **Add Honey and Mascarpone**: Drizzle the grilled peaches with honey and top with a dollop of mascarpone cheese.
5. **Garnish and Serve**: Garnish with fresh mint leaves and serve warm.

133. Grilled Bananas with Chocolate Sauce

Ingredients:

- 4 bananas, unpeeled and sliced lengthwise
- 1/4 cup melted butter
- 1/2 cup chocolate chips
- 1/4 cup heavy cream
- Whipped cream for serving

Instructions:

1. **Prepare Bananas**: Brush the cut sides of the bananas with melted butter.

2. **Preheat Griddle**: Heat the griddle to medium-high heat.

3. **Grill Bananas**: Place the bananas cut side down on the griddle and cook for 2-3 minutes, or until caramelized and softened.

4. **Make Chocolate Sauce**: In a small saucepan, heat the chocolate chips and heavy cream over low heat, stirring until melted and smooth.

5. **Serve**: Drizzle the grilled bananas with chocolate sauce and serve with whipped cream.

134. Grilled Apple Slices with Caramel Sauce

Ingredients:

- 4 large apples, cored and sliced into rings
- 2 tablespoons melted butter
- 1/4 cup caramel sauce
- 1/2 teaspoon ground cinnamon

Instructions:

1. **Prepare Apples**: Brush the apple slices with melted butter and sprinkle with cinnamon.

2. **Preheat Griddle**: Heat the griddle to medium-high heat.

3. **Grill Apples**: Place the apple slices on the griddle and cook for 2-3 minutes per side, or until tender and caramelized.

4. **Serve**: Drizzle with caramel sauce and serve warm.

135. Grilled Strawberries with Balsamic Glaze

Ingredients:

- 1 lb strawberries, hulled and halved
- 2 tablespoons balsamic vinegar

- 2 tablespoons honey
- Fresh basil leaves for garnish

Instructions:

1. **Prepare Strawberries**: In a bowl, toss the strawberries with balsamic vinegar and honey.
2. **Preheat Griddle**: Heat the griddle to medium-high heat.
3. **Grill Strawberries**: Place the strawberries on the griddle and cook for 1-2 minutes per side, or until softened and caramelized.
4. **Serve**: Garnish with fresh basil leaves and serve warm.

136. Grilled Pound Cake with Berries

Ingredients:

- 1 pound cake, sliced into thick slices
- 2 tablespoons melted butter
- 1 cup mixed berries (strawberries, blueberries, raspberries)
- 1/4 cup honey
- Whipped cream for serving

Instructions:

1. **Prepare Pound Cake**: Brush both sides of the pound cake slices with melted butter.
2. **Preheat Griddle**: Heat the griddle to medium-high heat.
3. **Grill Pound Cake**: Place the pound cake slices on the griddle and cook for 1-2 minutes per side, or until toasted and golden brown.
4. **Serve**: Top with mixed berries, drizzle with honey, and serve with whipped cream.

These six grilled fruits and desserts are easy to prepare and perfect for any occasion, adding a sweet and smoky twist to your meals. Enjoy these delightful treats with family and friends!

Gourmet Sweets

Elevate your dessert game with these gourmet sweets that are perfect for the grill. These recipes combine classic dessert flavors with the smoky, caramelized touch of grilling, creating unforgettable treats for any occasion.

137. Grilled S'mores

Ingredients:

- 8 graham crackers, halved
- 4 large marshmallows
- 2 chocolate bars, broken into squares

Instructions:

1. **Preheat Griddle**: Heat the griddle to medium heat.
2. **Grill Marshmallows**: Place the marshmallows on the griddle and cook for 1-2 minutes per side, until golden and gooey.
3. **Assemble S'mores**: Place a piece of chocolate on a graham cracker half, top with a grilled marshmallow, and cover with another graham cracker half.
4. **Serve**: Serve warm.

138. Grilled Lemon Pound Cake with Blueberry Compote

Ingredients:

- 1 lemon pound cake, sliced into thick slices
- 2 tablespoons melted butter
- 2 cups fresh blueberries
- 1/4 cup sugar
- 1 tablespoon lemon juice
- Whipped cream for serving

Instructions:

1. **Prepare Pound Cake**: Brush both sides of the pound cake slices with melted butter.

2. **Preheat Griddle**: Heat the griddle to medium-high heat.

3. **Grill Pound Cake**: Place the pound cake slices on the griddle and cook for 1-2 minutes per side, until toasted and golden brown.

4. **Make Blueberry Compote**: In a small saucepan, cook blueberries, sugar, and lemon juice over medium heat until the blueberries burst and the mixture thickens.

5. **Serve**: Serve the grilled pound cake with blueberry compote and whipped cream.

139. Grilled Mango with Lime and Chili

Ingredients:

- 2 ripe mangoes, peeled and sliced
- 2 tablespoons lime juice
- 1 teaspoon chili powder
- 2 tablespoons honey

Instructions:

1. **Prepare Mangoes**: Brush the mango slices with lime juice and sprinkle with chili powder.

2. **Preheat Griddle**: Heat the griddle to medium-high heat.

3. **Grill Mangoes**: Place the mango slices on the griddle and cook for 2-3 minutes per side, until caramelized.

4. **Serve**: Drizzle with honey and serve warm.

140. Grilled Chocolate-Dipped Strawberries

Ingredients:

- 1 lb strawberries, hulled
- 1 cup dark chocolate chips
- 2 tablespoons heavy cream

Instructions:

1. **Preheat Griddle**: Heat the griddle to medium-high heat.
2. **Grill Strawberries**: Place the strawberries on the griddle and cook for 1-2 minutes per side, until slightly softened.
3. **Make Chocolate Sauce**: In a small saucepan, melt the chocolate chips with heavy cream over low heat, stirring until smooth.
4. **Serve**: Dip the grilled strawberries in the chocolate sauce and serve immediately.

141. Grilled Pineapple Sundaes

Ingredients:

- 1 pineapple, peeled, cored, and sliced
- 2 tablespoons melted butter
- 1/4 cup brown sugar
- Vanilla ice cream for serving
- Caramel sauce for drizzling

Instructions:

1. **Prepare Pineapple**: Brush the pineapple slices with melted butter and sprinkle with brown sugar.
2. **Preheat Griddle**: Heat the griddle to medium-high heat.

3. **Grill Pineapple**: Place the pineapple slices on the griddle and cook for 2-3 minutes per side, until caramelized.

4. **Serve**: Serve the grilled pineapple with scoops of vanilla ice cream and a drizzle of caramel sauce.

142. Grilled Peaches with Amaretto

Ingredients:

- 4 ripe peaches, halved and pitted
- 2 tablespoons melted butter
- 1/4 cup Amaretto liqueur
- 1/4 cup brown sugar
- Whipped cream for serving

Instructions:

1. **Prepare Peaches**: Brush the peach halves with melted butter.
2. **Preheat Griddle**: Heat the griddle to medium-high heat.
3. **Grill Peaches**: Place the peaches cut side down on the griddle and cook for 3-4 minutes, until tender and caramelized.
4. **Add Amaretto and Sugar**: Drizzle with Amaretto and sprinkle with brown sugar.
5. **Serve**: Serve warm with whipped cream.

143. Grilled Apple Crisp

Ingredients:

- 4 large apples, cored and sliced
- 2 tablespoons melted butter
- 1/4 cup brown sugar
- 1 teaspoon ground cinnamon

- 1/2 cup granola

Instructions:

1. **Prepare Apples**: Brush the apple slices with melted butter and sprinkle with brown sugar and cinnamon.

2. **Preheat Griddle**: Heat the griddle to medium-high heat.

3. **Grill Apples**: Place the apple slices on the griddle and cook for 2-3 minutes per side, until tender and caramelized.

4. **Serve**: Serve the grilled apples topped with granola.

144. Grilled Banana Splits

Ingredients:

- 4 bananas, unpeeled and sliced lengthwise
- 2 tablespoons melted butter
- 1/4 cup chocolate chips
- 1/4 cup chopped nuts
- Vanilla ice cream for serving
- Whipped cream for serving

Instructions:

1. **Prepare Bananas**: Brush the cut sides of the bananas with melted butter.

2. **Preheat Griddle**: Heat the griddle to medium-high heat.

3. **Grill Bananas**: Place the bananas cut side down on the griddle and cook for 2-3 minutes, until caramelized and softened.

4. **Serve**: Serve the grilled bananas with scoops of vanilla ice cream, chocolate chips, chopped nuts, and whipped cream.

145. Grilled Figs with Goat Cheese and Honey

Ingredients:

- 8 fresh figs, halved
- 2 tablespoons olive oil
- 4 ounces goat cheese, crumbled
- 1/4 cup honey
- Fresh thyme leaves for garnish

Instructions:

1. **Prepare Figs**: Brush the fig halves with olive oil.
2. **Preheat Griddle**: Heat the griddle to medium-high heat.
3. **Grill Figs**: Place the figs cut side down on the griddle and cook for 2-3 minutes, until caramelized.
4. **Serve**: Top with crumbled goat cheese, drizzle with honey, and garnish with fresh thyme leaves.

146. Grilled Pears with Gorgonzola and Walnuts

Ingredients:

- 4 ripe pears, halved and cored
- 2 tablespoons olive oil
- 1/4 cup crumbled Gorgonzola cheese
- 1/4 cup chopped walnuts
- 2 tablespoons honey

Instructions:

1. **Prepare Pears**: Brush the pear halves with olive oil.
2. **Preheat Griddle**: Heat the griddle to medium-high heat.

3. **Grill Pears**: Place the pears cut side down on the griddle and cook for 3-4 minutes, until tender and caramelized.

4. **Serve**: Top with crumbled Gorgonzola cheese, chopped walnuts, and a drizzle of honey.

147. Grilled Plums with Honey and Almonds

Ingredients:

- 4 ripe plums, halved and pitted
- 2 tablespoons honey
- 1/4 cup sliced almonds
- 1/2 teaspoon ground cinnamon
- Fresh mint leaves for garnish

Instructions:

1. **Prepare Plums**: Brush the cut sides of the plums with honey.
2. **Preheat Griddle**: Heat the griddle to medium-high heat.
3. **Grill Plums**: Place the plums cut side down on the griddle and cook for 3-4 minutes, until tender and caramelized.
4. **Add Almonds and Cinnamon**: Sprinkle with sliced almonds and cinnamon.
5. **Serve**: Garnish with fresh mint leaves and serve warm.

148. Grilled Nectarines with Ricotta and Honey

Ingredients:

- 4 ripe nectarines, halved and pitted
- 1/2 cup ricotta cheese
- 2 tablespoons honey
- 1 teaspoon vanilla extract

- Fresh basil leaves for garnish

Instructions:

1. **Prepare Nectarines**: Brush the cut sides of the nectarines with a little honey.

2. **Preheat Griddle**: Heat the griddle to medium-high heat.

3. **Grill Nectarines**: Place the nectarines cut side down on the griddle and cook for 3-4 minutes, until tender and caramelized.

4. **Prepare Ricotta Mixture**: In a bowl, mix ricotta cheese, honey, and vanilla extract.

5. **Serve**: Top each grilled nectarine half with a spoonful of the ricotta mixture. Garnish with fresh basil leaves and serve warm.

149. Grilled Pineapple and Coconut Rum Cake

Ingredients:

- 1 pineapple, peeled, cored, and sliced
- 2 tablespoons melted butter
- 1/4 cup coconut rum
- 1/4 cup shredded coconut
- 1 coconut cake, sliced

Instructions:

1. **Prepare Pineapple**: Brush the pineapple slices with melted butter and coconut rum.

2. **Preheat Griddle**: Heat the griddle to medium-high heat.

3. **Grill Pineapple**: Place the pineapple slices on the griddle and cook for 2-3 minutes per side, until caramelized.

4. **Toast Coconut**: In a small pan, toast the shredded coconut until golden brown.

5. **Serve**: Serve the grilled pineapple on top of slices of coconut cake, sprinkled with toasted coconut.

150. Grilled Watermelon with Feta and Mint

Ingredients:

- 8 watermelon wedges
- 2 tablespoons olive oil
- 1/4 cup crumbled feta cheese
- Fresh mint leaves for garnish

Instructions:

1. **Prepare Watermelon**: Brush the watermelon wedges with olive oil.
2. **Preheat Griddle**: Heat the griddle to medium-high heat.
3. **Grill Watermelon**: Place the watermelon wedges on the griddle and cook for 1-2 minutes per side, until grill marks appear.
4. **Serve**: Sprinkle with crumbled feta cheese and garnish with fresh mint leaves. Serve immediately.

151. Grilled Ananas with Ice Cream and Caramel Sauce

Ingredients:

- 1 pineapple, peeled, cored, and sliced into rings
- 2 tablespoons melted butter
- 1/2 cup caramel sauce
- Vanilla ice cream for serving

Instructions:

1. **Prepare Pineapple**: Brush the pineapple rings with melted butter.
2. **Preheat Griddle**: Heat the griddle to medium-high heat.
3. **Grill Pineapple**: Place the pineapple rings on the griddle and cook for 2-3 minutes per side, until caramelized.

4. **Serve**: Serve the grilled pineapple rings with scoops of vanilla ice cream and drizzle with caramel sauce.

These gourmet sweets are perfect for grilling, offering a delightful combination of flavors and textures that will impress your guests and satisfy your sweet tooth. Enjoy these delicious grilled desserts at your next gathering or as a special treat!

Chapter 8: Irresistible Sauces and Marinades

Enhance your grilling experience with these irresistible sauces and marinades. Each one brings out the best in your grilled dishes, adding depth, flavor, and excitement to your meals. Here are some recipes to get you started:

Sauces

1. Classic BBQ Sauce

Ingredients:

- 1 cup ketchup
- 1/4 cup apple cider vinegar
- 1/4 cup brown sugar
- 2 tablespoons Worcestershire sauce
- 1 tablespoon Dijon mustard
- 2 teaspoons smoked paprika
- 1 teaspoon garlic powder
- Salt and pepper to taste

Instructions:

1. **Mix Ingredients**: In a bowl, combine all ingredients and mix well.

2. **Simmer**: Transfer the mixture to a saucepan and simmer over medium heat for 10-15 minutes, until thickened.
3. **Serve**: Use immediately or store in the refrigerator for up to a week.

2. Chimichurri Sauce

Ingredients:

- 1 cup fresh parsley, finely chopped
- 1/2 cup fresh cilantro, finely chopped
- 1/4 cup red wine vinegar
- 1/2 cup olive oil
- 4 cloves garlic, minced
- 1 teaspoon dried oregano
- 1/2 teaspoon red pepper flakes
- Salt and pepper to taste

Instructions:

1. **Combine Ingredients**: In a bowl, mix all ingredients until well combined.
2. **Adjust Seasoning**: Adjust salt and pepper to taste.
3. **Serve**: Serve immediately or store in the refrigerator for up to 3 days.

3. Honey Mustard Sauce

Ingredients:

- 1/2 cup Dijon mustard
- 1/4 cup honey
- 2 tablespoons apple cider vinegar
- 1/4 cup mayonnaise

- Salt and pepper to taste

Instructions:

1. **Mix Ingredients**: In a bowl, whisk together Dijon mustard, honey, apple cider vinegar, and mayonnaise.

2. **Adjust Seasoning**: Add salt and pepper to taste.

3. **Serve**: Serve immediately or store in the refrigerator for up to a week.

4. Spicy Sriracha Mayo

Ingredients:

- 1/2 cup mayonnaise
- 2 tablespoons Sriracha sauce
- 1 tablespoon lime juice
- 1 clove garlic, minced

Instructions:

1. **Combine Ingredients**: In a bowl, mix mayonnaise, Sriracha sauce, lime juice, and minced garlic.

2. **Adjust Seasoning**: Adjust the amount of Sriracha to taste.

3. **Serve**: Serve immediately or store in the refrigerator for up to a week.

5. Teriyaki Sauce

Ingredients:

- 1/2 cup soy sauce
- 1/4 cup brown sugar
- 2 tablespoons mirin
- 1 tablespoon rice vinegar
- 2 cloves garlic, minced

- 1 teaspoon grated ginger

Instructions:

1. **Mix Ingredients**: In a saucepan, combine soy sauce, brown sugar, mirin, rice vinegar, garlic, and ginger.

2. **Simmer**: Bring to a simmer over medium heat and cook for 5-7 minutes, until slightly thickened.

3. **Serve**: Use immediately or store in the refrigerator for up to a week.

6. Tzatziki Sauce

Ingredients:

- 1 cup Greek yogurt
- 1 cucumber, grated and drained
- 2 cloves garlic, minced
- 1 tablespoon lemon juice
- 1 tablespoon fresh dill, chopped
- Salt and pepper to taste

Instructions:

1. **Combine Ingredients**: In a bowl, mix Greek yogurt, grated cucumber, garlic, lemon juice, and dill.

2. **Adjust Seasoning**: Add salt and pepper to taste.

3. **Serve**: Serve immediately or store in the refrigerator for up to 3 days.

7. Mango Salsa

Ingredients:

- 2 ripe mangoes, diced
- 1/4 cup red onion, finely chopped

- 1/4 cup red bell pepper, finely chopped
- 1 jalapeño, seeded and minced
- 1/4 cup fresh cilantro, chopped
- Juice of 1 lime
- Salt to taste

Instructions:

1. **Combine Ingredients**: In a bowl, mix mangoes, red onion, red bell pepper, jalapeño, cilantro, and lime juice.
2. **Adjust Seasoning**: Add salt to taste.
3. **Serve**: Serve immediately or store in the refrigerator for up to 2 days.

8. Garlic Herb Butter

Ingredients:

- 1/2 cup unsalted butter, softened
- 2 cloves garlic, minced
- 1 tablespoon fresh parsley, chopped
- 1 tablespoon fresh thyme, chopped
- 1 tablespoon fresh rosemary, chopped
- Salt and pepper to taste

Instructions:

1. **Mix Ingredients**: In a bowl, combine softened butter, garlic, parsley, thyme, rosemary, salt, and pepper.
2. **Chill**: Transfer to a piece of plastic wrap, form into a log, and chill in the refrigerator until firm.

3. **Serve**: Slice and serve with grilled meats or vegetables.

---

9. Pesto Sauce

Ingredients:

- 2 cups fresh basil leaves
- 1/2 cup grated Parmesan cheese
- 1/3 cup pine nuts
- 2 cloves garlic
- 1/2 cup olive oil
- Salt and pepper to taste

Instructions:

1. **Blend Ingredients**: In a food processor, combine basil, Parmesan cheese, pine nuts, and garlic. Blend until finely chopped.
2. **Add Oil**: With the processor running, slowly add olive oil until the mixture is smooth.
3. **Adjust Seasoning**: Add salt and pepper to taste.
4. **Serve**: Use immediately or store in the refrigerator for up to a week.

---

10. Lemon Dill Sauce

Ingredients:

- 1/2 cup sour cream
- 2 tablespoons fresh dill, chopped
- 1 tablespoon lemon juice
- 1 teaspoon lemon zest
- Salt and pepper to taste

Instructions:

1. **Combine Ingredients**: In a bowl, mix sour cream, dill, lemon juice, lemon zest, salt, and pepper.

2. **Adjust Seasoning**: Add more lemon juice or zest if desired.

3. **Serve**: Serve immediately or store in the refrigerator for up to 3 days.

Marinades

1. Classic Italian Marinade

Ingredients:

- 1/2 cup olive oil
- 1/4 cup red wine vinegar
- 2 cloves garlic, minced
- 1 tablespoon dried oregano
- 1 tablespoon dried basil
- 1 teaspoon salt
- 1/2 teaspoon black pepper

Instructions:

1. **Combine Ingredients**: In a bowl, mix olive oil, red wine vinegar, garlic, oregano, basil, salt, and pepper.

2. **Marinate**: Pour over vegetables or proteins and marinate for at least 30 minutes before grilling.

2. Spicy Chipotle Marinade

Ingredients:

- 1/4 cup olive oil
- 2 tablespoons lime juice

- 2 tablespoons chipotle peppers in adobo sauce, minced
- 2 cloves garlic, minced
- 1 teaspoon ground cumin
- 1 teaspoon smoked paprika
- Salt and pepper to taste

Instructions:

1. **Combine Ingredients**: In a bowl, mix olive oil, lime juice, chipotle peppers, garlic, cumin, smoked paprika, salt, and pepper.
2. **Marinate**: Pour over vegetables or proteins and marinate for at least 30 minutes before grilling.

3. Asian Sesame Marinade

Ingredients:

- 1/4 cup soy sauce
- 2 tablespoons sesame oil
- 2 tablespoons rice vinegar
- 1 tablespoon honey
- 1 tablespoon grated ginger
- 2 cloves garlic, minced
- 1 tablespoon sesame seeds

Instructions:

1. **Combine Ingredients**: In a bowl, mix soy sauce, sesame oil, rice vinegar, honey, ginger, garlic, and sesame seeds.
2. **Marinate**: Pour over vegetables or proteins and marinate for at least 30 minutes before grilling.

4. Mediterranean Lemon Marinade

Ingredients:

- 1/4 cup olive oil
- 2 tablespoons lemon juice
- 1 tablespoon lemon zest
- 2 cloves garlic, minced
- 1 teaspoon dried thyme
- 1 teaspoon dried rosemary
- Salt and pepper to taste

Instructions:

1. **Combine Ingredients**: In a bowl, mix olive oil, lemon juice, lemon zest, garlic, thyme, rosemary, salt, and pepper.
2. **Marinate**: Pour over vegetables or proteins and marinate for at least 30 minutes before grilling.

5. Sweet and Tangy Teriyaki Marinade

Ingredients:

- 1/4 cup soy sauce
- 2 tablespoons mirin
- 2 tablespoons brown sugar
- 1 tablespoon rice vinegar
- 1 clove garlic, minced
- 1 teaspoon grated ginger

Instructions:

1. **Combine Ingredients**: In a bowl, mix soy sauce, mirin, brown sugar, rice vinegar, garlic, and ginger.

2. **Marinate**: Pour over vegetables or proteins and marinate for at least 30 minutes before grilling.

6. Garlic Herb Marinade

Ingredients:

- 1/4 cup olive oil
- 2 tablespoons red wine vinegar
- 2 cloves garlic, minced
- 1 tablespoon fresh rosemary, chopped
- 1 tablespoon fresh thyme, chopped
- Salt and pepper to taste

Instructions:

1. **Combine Ingredients**: In a bowl, mix olive oil, red wine vinegar, garlic, rosemary, thyme, salt, and pepper.
2. **Marinate**: Pour over vegetables or proteins and marinate for at least 30 minutes before grilling.

7. Jamaican Jerk Marinade

Ingredients:

- 1/4 cup olive oil
- 2 tablespoons lime juice
- 2 tablespoons soy sauce
- 2 cloves garlic, minced
- 1 tablespoon brown sugar

- 1 tablespoon jerk seasoning
- 1 teaspoon ground allspice

Instructions:

1. **Combine Ingredients**: In a bowl, mix olive oil, lime juice, soy sauce, garlic, brown sugar, jerk seasoning, and allspice.
2. **Marinate**: Pour over vegetables or proteins and marinate for at least 30 minutes before grilling.

8. Balsamic Rosemary Marinade

Ingredients:

- 1/4 cup balsamic vinegar
- 2 tablespoons olive oil
- 2 cloves garlic, minced
- 1 tablespoon fresh rosemary, chopped
- 1 tablespoon Dijon mustard
- Salt and pepper to taste

Instructions:

1. **Combine Ingredients**: In a bowl, mix balsamic vinegar, olive oil, garlic, rosemary, Dijon mustard, salt, and pepper.
2. **Marinate**: Pour over vegetables or proteins and marinate for at least 30 minutes before grilling.

9. Smoky Paprika Marinade

Ingredients:

- 1/4 cup olive oil
- 2 tablespoons apple cider vinegar

- 1 tablespoon smoked paprika
- 2 cloves garlic, minced
- 1 teaspoon ground cumin
- Salt and pepper to taste

Instructions:

1. **Combine Ingredients**: In a bowl, mix olive oil, apple cider vinegar, smoked paprika, garlic, cumin, salt, and pepper.
2. **Marinate**: Pour over vegetables or proteins and marinate for at least 30 minutes before grilling.

10. Thai Coconut Marinade

Ingredients:

- 1/4 cup coconut milk
- 2 tablespoons lime juice
- 1 tablespoon soy sauce
- 1 tablespoon brown sugar
- 1 clove garlic, minced
- 1 teaspoon grated ginger
- 1 teaspoon red curry paste

Instructions:

1. **Combine Ingredients**: In a bowl, mix coconut milk, lime juice, soy sauce, brown sugar, garlic, ginger, and red curry paste.
2. **Marinate**: Pour over vegetables or proteins and marinate for at least 30 minutes before grilling.

These sauces and marinades will add a burst of flavor to your grilled dishes, making them even more delicious and memorable. Enjoy experimenting with these recipes and finding your favorites!

Appendix

Conversions and Measurements

Cooking, especially grilling, often requires precise measurements and conversions to ensure the best results. This section provides essential conversion tables and measurement guidelines to help you navigate your recipes with ease.

Volume Conversions:

- 1 teaspoon (tsp) = 5 milliliters (ml)
- 1 tablespoon (tbsp) = 15 milliliters (ml)
- 1 fluid ounce (fl oz) = 30 milliliters (ml)
- 1 cup (c) = 240 milliliters (ml)
- 1 pint (pt) = 2 cups (480 milliliters)
- 1 quart (qt) = 4 cups (960 milliliters)
- 1 gallon (gal) = 4 quarts (3.8 liters)

Weight Conversions:

- 1 ounce (oz) = 28 grams (g)
- 1 pound (lb) = 16 ounces (oz) = 454 grams (g)

Temperature Conversions:

- **To convert Fahrenheit (°F) to Celsius (°C):** $°C = (°F - 32) \times \frac{5}{9}$
- **To convert Celsius (°C) to Fahrenheit (°F):** $°F = °C \times \frac{9}{5} + 32$

Common Cooking Measurements:

- **Pinch:** A small amount, usually less than 1/8 teaspoon.
- **Dash:** Approximately 1/8 teaspoon.
- **1/4 teaspoon:** Approximately 1.25 milliliters.
- **1/2 teaspoon:** Approximately 2.5 milliliters.
- **1 teaspoon:** Approximately 5 milliliters.
- **1 tablespoon:** Approximately 15 milliliters.

Dry Ingredient Equivalents:

- **1 cup all-purpose flour:** Approximately 120 grams.
- **1 cup granulated sugar:** Approximately 200 grams.
- **1 cup brown sugar, packed:** Approximately 220 grams.
- **1 cup powdered sugar:** Approximately 120 grams.
- **1 cup butter:** 2 sticks or 8 ounces (226 grams).

Understanding these conversions and measurements can make a significant difference in the success of your recipes. Whether you're scaling a recipe up or down, these guidelines will help ensure accuracy and consistency in your cooking.

Ingredient Substitutions

Sometimes, you might not have a specific ingredient on hand, or you may need to accommodate dietary restrictions. Here are some common ingredient substitutions to help you adapt recipes without compromising on taste or texture.

Baking Substitutions:

- **Buttermilk:** For 1 cup of buttermilk, substitute with 1 cup of milk plus 1 tablespoon of lemon juice or white vinegar. Let it sit for 5 minutes before using.
- **Baking Powder:** For 1 teaspoon of baking powder, substitute with 1/4 teaspoon baking soda plus 1/2 teaspoon cream of tartar.
- **Eggs:** For 1 egg, substitute with 1/4 cup unsweetened applesauce or 1 tablespoon ground flaxseed mixed with 3 tablespoons water (let it sit for 5 minutes).

Dairy Substitutions:

- **Heavy Cream:** For 1 cup of heavy cream, substitute with 3/4 cup milk plus 1/3 cup melted butter.

- **Sour Cream:** For 1 cup of sour cream, substitute with 1 cup plain Greek yogurt.

- **Milk:** For 1 cup of milk, substitute with 1 cup almond milk, soy milk, or oat milk.

Sweetener Substitutions:

- **Granulated Sugar:** For 1 cup of granulated sugar, substitute with 3/4 cup honey or 3/4 cup maple syrup (reduce other liquids in the recipe by 1/4 cup).

- **Brown Sugar:** For 1 cup of brown sugar, substitute with 1 cup granulated sugar plus 1 tablespoon molasses.

- **Powdered Sugar:** For 1 cup of powdered sugar, blend 1 cup granulated sugar with 1 tablespoon cornstarch until fine.

Flavor Enhancers:

- **Vanilla Extract:** For 1 teaspoon of vanilla extract, substitute with 1 teaspoon of almond extract or 1 teaspoon of maple syrup.

- **Fresh Herbs:** For 1 tablespoon of fresh herbs, substitute with 1 teaspoon of dried herbs.

These substitutions can help you maintain the integrity of your dishes while accommodating different ingredients you have on hand or catering to dietary needs. Experimenting with substitutions can also lead to new and exciting flavors in your recipes.

Conclusion

Become a Griddle Master

Congratulations on embarking on this culinary journey with the Gas Griddle Cookbook! By now, you've explored a diverse array of recipes, from savory meats to delectable desserts, and learned essential grilling techniques, sauces, marinades, and vegetarian dishes. The path to becoming a griddle master is paved with practice, experimentation, and a passion for delicious food. Here are some final tips and insights to help you on your way to griddle mastery.

Embrace the Basics

Mastering the basics is the foundation of any great chef. Ensure you understand the fundamental grilling techniques, such as direct and indirect heat, the importance of preheating your griddle, and the art of timing. Always start with a clean griddle to avoid unwanted flavors and ensure even cooking. Familiarize yourself with different cooking oils and their smoke points to choose the best one for your dishes.

Experiment with Flavors

Don't be afraid to experiment with flavors and ingredients. The beauty of grilling lies in its versatility. Try different marinades and rubs, explore international cuisines, and mix and match your favorite ingredients. Use the sauces and marinades section as a starting point, but feel free to tweak the recipes to suit your taste. Grilling is as much about creativity as it is about technique.

Pay Attention to Details

Details matter when it comes to grilling. Pay attention to the thickness of your cuts, the temperature of your griddle, and the internal temperature of your meats. Use a meat thermometer to ensure your meats are cooked to perfection. Resting your meats after grilling is crucial to lock in juices and flavors. Simple steps like these can elevate your dishes from good to exceptional.

Stay Safe

Grilling can be a fun and rewarding experience, but safety should always come first. Always use heat-resistant gloves and utensils, keep a fire extinguisher nearby, and never leave your griddle unattended. Be cautious with marinades and sauces containing sugar, as they can cause flare-ups. Regularly check for gas leaks and ensure your grill is in good working condition.

Share Your Creations

One of the joys of grilling is sharing your delicious creations with friends and family. Host BBQ parties, share your favorite recipes, and enjoy the communal aspect of cooking outdoors. Take pride in your progress and don't hesitate to show off your newfound skills. Food has a unique way of bringing people together, and your grilled masterpieces can create lasting memories.

Keep Learning

The journey to becoming a griddle master never truly ends. Keep learning and improving your skills by trying new recipes, attending grilling workshops, and staying updated with the latest grilling techniques and trends. There are countless resources available, from cooking shows and books to online forums and social media groups, where you can connect with fellow grilling enthusiasts and learn from their experiences.

Enjoy the Process

Most importantly, enjoy the process. Grilling is not just about the end result but also about the experience of cooking outdoors, experimenting with flavors, and savoring the aromas. Embrace the challenges and celebrate the successes. Each grilling session is an opportunity to refine your skills and discover new favorites.

Final Thoughts

Thank you for choosing the Gas Griddle Cookbook as your guide to mastering the art of grilling. Whether you're a novice or an experienced griller, this book is designed to inspire and equip you with the knowledge and confidence to create delicious meals on your gas griddle. Remember, the key to becoming a griddle master is practice, patience, and a genuine love for cooking.

So, fire up your griddle, gather your ingredients, and embark on a culinary adventure. The world of grilling awaits you, and with the skills and recipes you've acquired, you're well on your way to becoming a true griddle master. Happy grilling!

www.ingramcontent.com/pod-product-compliance
Lightning Source LLC
Chambersburg PA
CBHW082209070526
44585CB00020B/2345